The Art and Science
of Lesson Design

The Art and Science of Lesson Design

Practical Approaches to Boosting Cognitive Rigor in the Classroom

John R. Walkup
With Stephan Squire

ROWMAN & LITTLEFIELD
Lanham • Boulder • New York • London

Published by Rowman & Littlefield
An imprint of The Rowman & Littlefield Publishing Group, Inc.
4501 Forbes Boulevard, Suite 200, Lanham, Maryland 20706
www.rowman.com

6 Tinworth Street, London SE11 5AL, United Kingdom

Copyright © 2020 by The Rowman & Littlefield Publishing Group, Inc

All rights reserved. No part of this book may be reproduced in any form or by any electronic or mechanical means, including information storage and retrieval systems, without written permission from the publisher, except by a reviewer who may quote passages in a review.

British Library Cataloguing in Publication Information Available

Library of Congress Cataloging-in-Publication Data

Includes bibliographic references and index.
ISBN 978-1-4758-5442-8 (cloth)
ISBN 978-1-4758-5443-5 (pbk.)
ISBN 978-1-4758-5444-2 (Electronic)

Contents

Preface ... ix
    Problems with Education ... x
    My Search for Something Better ... x
    What Should We Teach? ... xii
    How Should We Teach? ... xiii
    Goal ... xiv

Acknowledgments ... xv

Introduction ... xvii
    Critical Features of a Lesson ... xviii
    What is Rigor? ... xix
    Terminology ... xxi
    Depth of Knowledge (DOK) ... xxi
    Cognitive Process Dimension (CPD) of Bloom's Taxonomy ... xxiii
    Enter Cognitive Rigor ... xxvii
    Knowledge Dimension of Bloom's Taxonomy ... xxvii
    The Taxonomy Table ... xxx
    The Rigor Cube ... xxx
    What Do We Want to Achieve? ... xxxi

1 Lesson Scope ... 1
    State Content Standards and Topics ... 1
    Choosing a Career Focus ... 4
    Sample Lessons ... 6
    What's Next? ... 10

2 Culminating Activity ... 11
    Creating a Culminating Activity ... 11

	Learning Objectives	16
	Language Objectives	17
	Sample Lessons	17
	What's Next?	21
3	Lesson Content	23
	Grade-Appropriate Content	23
	Background Barriers	28
	Sample Lessons	28
	What's Next?	36
4	Lesson Delivery Methods	39
	Impact of the CPD	39
	Alternative Bloom's Verbs	40
	Mapping Instructional Methods to the CPD	41
	Sample Lessons	41
	Professional Development	57
	What's Next?	57
5	Background Barriers	59
	Need for Subskill Scaffolding	60
	Proficiency Defined	60
	Subskill Scaffolding	62
	Proficiency on State Tests	65
	Sample Lessons	66
	Fine-Tuning	74
	Reflection	75
	What's Next?	76
6	Formative Assessment	77
	Checking for Understanding	78
	Questioning for Engagement	79
	Developing Questions	80
	Delivering Questions	82
	Homework	88
	Sample Lessons	91
7	Vignette	95
	Step 1	95
	Step 2	96
	Step 3	97
	Step 4	99
	Step 5	102
	Delivery Order	103
	Homework	103

Appendix A: Instructional Strategies   105
    Cognitive Strategies   105
    Gradual Release of Responsibility (GRR)   106
    I Do, We Do, You Do   107
    Think-Alouds   108
    Socratic Seminars   109
    Guided Inquiry   110
    Metacognition Question Bank   111
    Metacog Log   112

Appendix B: Templates   113

References   115

Index   121

Preface

As a professional educator, I prepare every day to teach topics I find interesting and sometimes even exciting. Much of my fulfillment comes from students finding my lessons similarly engaging. Because pedagogy is my craft, the disappointment I feel when students fail to respond to my instruction digs deep into my psyche. I am sure many of you feel the same way.

There is nothing more satisfying to educators than to see students respond to a lesson and later demonstrate mastery of what they learned. To meet this goal, they need expertise in developing engaging, stimulating classroom environments. The art and science of teaching requires considerable training, stimulating collaboration, and a steady stream of new ideas.

Most of what I know about pedagogy I learned from teachers like you. I have stepped into hundreds of classrooms over the past decade to observe daily instruction and discuss instructional strategy with teachers. In many cases, teachers pointed out flaws in my own philosophy and showed me ways they used their own instincts to enrich the classroom environment. Naturally, I absorbed these ideas into my own skill set.

I am an educator, working mostly at the university level along with a short stint as a public high school teacher in Oklahoma. Around 2003, I began my consulting career as a workshop trainer and classroom observer for a company in California's Central Valley. They promoted a strict teacher-centered outlook based on direct instruction (not to be confused with Direct Instruction, a specific teaching method involving teachers following a script). Their attitude was that they knew best, and that our nation's learners would no longer struggle if only teachers would do as they say. As a faithful employee, I adopted a similar stance and soon began to dismiss more progressive approaches as ineffective and hopelessly idealistic.

One day, an assistant superintendent in Hartford, Connecticut, took me to task for my narrow, arrogant views. On the plane flight home, I began to rethink my approach. By the end of the flight, I had decided to view instruction through a different lens. So, I jumped ship in 2007 to form The Standards Company, an education research and professional development company located in Clovis, California. I was lucky to have on my team a staff of dedicated thinkers. With their input, I quickly set out to reinvent the manner in which the educational community looks at curriculum and instruction.

PROBLEMS WITH EDUCATION

To me, it appears that the education field is awash with ideas from the burgeoning pop education book market and social media. Many of these ideas are founded on Pollyanna notions of child psychology and driven by the educator's personal politics. Common sense and reasoning often lose out in the movement to be seen as open-minded and progressive.

Quite often an educator offers something worthwhile. What education lacks, however, is a practical approach to infuse these ideas into daily instruction. As I see it, we need a systematic process for developing lesson plans that leverages the most powerful tools available to educators. Rather than promote a single way to teach, *this approach should allow flexibility for you to incorporate those methods that have worked best in your own classroom.*

MY SEARCH FOR SOMETHING BETTER

Shortly after forming The Standards Company, I began looking for ways to improve curriculum analysis, which I had decided would form the cornerstone of the company's mission. I was aware of Bloom's taxonomy already, but my initial attempts to assess the rigor of curricular materials through its lens fell short. Although Bloom's taxonomy had benefited from widespread adoption, it alone appeared insufficient for categorizing curricular quality. I soon began searching for a better schema and found the Depth of Knowledge levels of Norman Webb. Rather than dropping Bloom's taxonomy, I decided that both provided meaningful utility in the curriculum analysis field.

Teachers had grown accustomed to Bloom's taxonomy since its inception in the 1950s, but around 2008 Depth of Knowledge began capturing much of the discussion on curriculum development and instruction. Some educators surmised that Depth of Knowledge was designed to replace Bloom's taxonomy, while others figured they were both manifestations of the same scheme. Even those able to distinguish the two often struggled to understand how to actually use these constructs in the classroom.

By superposing both Bloom's taxonomy and Depth of Knowledge levels into a common framework, my company helped create the concept of Cognitive Rigor and its associated tool called the Cognitive Rigor Matrix. I then began to see that within its structure, Cognitive Rigor offered a powerful tool for driving instruction at the classroom level, from lesson planning and delivery to student assessment.

Impact of Cognitive Rigor

Unbeknownst to me and my company, an education consultant in New Hampshire named Karin Hess had already developed a model similar to Cognitive Rigor for use in aligning curricular content to state tests and standards. At the suggestion of Norman Webb, Karin Hess and my company convened to discuss our achievements. We then teamed up in October 2007 to introduce the concept of Cognitive Rigor and the Cognitive Rigor Matrix to the public, culminating in an article titled "Cognitive Rigor: Blending the Strengths of Bloom's Taxonomy and Webb's Depth of Knowledge to Enhance Classroom-level Processes." Today, this article is widely distributed online and cited. (See the Bibliography for information on obtaining this article.)

Since its introduction, the Cognitive Rigor Matrix has found wide use at all levels of school governance. Some of the more notable adopters of the matrix include the following:

- The Oklahoma State Department of Education commissioned use of the Cognitive Rigor matrix to evaluate the rigor of student assignments collected from 3,600 school teachers for all K-12 grade levels.
- The Nevada State Legislature similarly commissioned use of the matrix for its own state study involving 3,500 teachers in grades 3–8.
- The Smarter Balanced Assessment Consortium (SBAC) has adopted its use to select test items for its SBAC statewide assessments.
- The California Department of Education uses the concept of Cognitive Rigor as a foundational resource for implementing the Next Generation Science Standards.
- The New York City Department of Education uses the matrix as an integral component of its WeTeachNYC professional development program for teachers.
- The Northwest Evaluation Association uses the Cognitive Rigor Matrix to align its Measures of Academic Progress (MAP) assessment items to Next Generation Science Standards.

- The Pennsylvania Department of Education used the Cognitive Rigor Matrix in 2010 to align its academic standards to the new Common Core State Standards in mathematics and English language arts.

The power of Cognitive Rigor in driving lesson plan development has only begun to surface in the education literature. I wrote this book to promote the use of Cognitive Rigor to a wider audience.

I will soon present to you a systematic approach toward taking that next step with Cognitive Rigor—using it to develop lessons that stimulate a wide range of cognitive complexity. These lessons will incorporate topics that span numerous disciplines. This approach will also provide you a means for selecting optimal instructional delivery techniques. Just as importantly, your lessons will incorporate effective techniques for assessing student proficiency continually throughout lesson delivery. I will also devote a special section to discuss how to accommodate those students who lack background knowledge/skills into the same rigorous learning environment as their peers.

WHAT SHOULD WE TEACH?

State content standards were initially developed because many felt that the curriculum experienced by students should be standardized to the choice of topics. The idea is that no matter their career aspirations, students need to learn a progression of topics beginning in the earliest years. Otherwise, the enacted curriculum will tend to overly focus on topics favored by the teacher and not what is needed.

State content standards also addressed the depth to which the education community felt were reasonable levels of rigor. Rather than simply listing topics, standards writers infused the standards with action verbs designed to compel teachers to drill deeper into content. For example, it was no longer enough for a teacher to merely cover metaphors—standards-based instruction compelled teachers to teach students to define metaphors, identify them in sentences, analyze their meaning, and even create metaphors that met certain criteria.

The debate on whether students should be taught grade-appropriate content surfaces constantly. Consider the following sentiment that is not uncommon in public education, especially in schools with high dropout rates:

> I don't teach on grade-level. Face it, the students here don't go to college. I focus on real-world skills, the stuff that they will help them get and keep jobs.

We should acknowledge that if students decide not to go to college, that should be *their* decision. If we teach off-grade level, we are in effect making that decision for them. Withholding grade-appropriate content therefore deprives students of knowledge expressed in the state content standards that the public has, through their state board of education, declared rightfully theirs. Such a practice effectively places an artificial cap on their learning.

HOW SHOULD WE TEACH?

"Tastes Great!"
"Less Filling!"
"Ginger!"
"Mary Ann!"

Just like these debates of yesteryear, the educational community still tends to form into warring camps. The Phonics Brigade has long battled the Whole Language Cavalry over the best way to teach reading. Math instruction is equally polarized. Old Math has continually squared off against New Math, the New New Math, and now a host of progressive approaches spurred by the Common Core. Most pertinent to our lesson planning, the teacher-centered camp (i.e., traditional instruction) has battled the student-centered camp (i.e., progressive instruction) over the "best way to teach."

I think this is all a bit silly.

A vibrant classroom lesson features the teacher diving in and out of various instructional methods—sometimes the teacher leads the learning and other times the students lead the learning. Direct instruction might surface at some point in the lesson followed by a Socratic seminar, then perhaps followed by a stint in guided inquiry. Or, maybe the entire lesson will employ Gradual Release of Responsibility. The choice is up to you, the teacher.

I was trained in the past to push the teacher-centered approach hard, writing off student-centered approaches as inefficient drivel. Today, I would no more expect you to enlist in the teacher-centered camp (or in the student-centered camp for that matter) than I would expect a group of diners to adopt a fork-only policy. In this book, we pay equal respect to both student- and teacher-centered instruction, therefore remaining neutral in the pedagogy wars.

To many researchers and educators, however, there is still a "best method" out there awaiting discovery. Once found, all will be good. But they are wrong. You are free to choose from a wide range of instructional methods at your disposal, each of which works well in some situations but not others. You can even develop entirely new methods of your own. If so, you will find the approach to lesson planning offered in this book a perfect vehicle for deploying them.

GOAL

It is my goal that reading this book will boost your confidence in developing lesson plans that students find highly satisfying and rewarding. You will be able to discuss at length some of the tools used in curriculum development that have generated so much attention but for which many do not truly understand how to apply at the classroom level.

In the end, I hope you use your newly learned skills to help your colleagues develop a clear roadmap toward reaching school-wide goals for improving student learning. The ideas presented here may require a more concerted effort on your part to absorb than the usual collection of mere tips and techniques. But nothing worthwhile is easy.

Acknowledgments

John Walkup and Stephon Squire thank Erik Francis for numerous enlightening conversations on Cognitive Rigor over the past few years. They also thank Eric Madrigal, Rabdeep Shergill, Bibiana Orozco, Skylar Nguyen, and Michael Walkup for their suggestions on improving the manuscript. Finally, John Walkup thank Ben Jones for his remarkable insights and expertise and John Pilipenko for his outstanding management and technical skills.

Introduction

This chapter will introduce the concept of Cognitive Rigor (Hess et al. 2009) and its development. Its associated Cognitive Rigor Matrix (also called the Hess Matrix) will serve as our foundation for a powerful and innovative lesson planning approach to K-12 instruction. The subject-specific examples called Hess CRMs that were developed by Karin Hess (2014) will further aid our efforts (Hess 2018, Hess 2019). Then, we will discuss how we can supplement the Cognitive Rigor Matrix to form a three-dimensional model called the Rigor Cube, which will drive our lesson development process.

The lessons we will develop using the Rigor Cube will adhere to certain principles and characteristics:

- In much the same fashion as problem-based learning (PBL), culminating activities will guide students through the learning process.
- Lesson plans will accommodate teachers that favor traditional instruction as well as those that want to employ more progressive techniques; in fact, most lessons will blend both instructional approaches.
- Proficiency will be tightly defined so as to emphasize grade-level content and avoid evaluating them on background knowledge.
- Instruction will target the whole class, leaving no student out of the learning process.
- Relevance and communication will be explicitly inserted into the lesson plan.
- Our goal is not to stamp out low-rigor lessons or assignments. Rather, we strive for students to experience a wider range of rigor throughout the semester.

CRITICAL FEATURES OF A LESSON

Lesson planning has grown ever more complex as teachers face an increasing number of challenges in the classroom. At some point, it is wise to step back and rethink our approach. The approach favored in this book targets three goals of learning that combine to span the gamut of subjects and topics, as illustrated in figure I.1:

1. Academic content—the traditional mark of an educated person is one who *knows* and *knows how*. Students who must perform an online search to learn the significance of Pearl Harbor have not yet been adequately educated in American history. Students who cannot solve for x in an equation have not yet been adequately educated in math. As such, this book will avoid joining the movement to cast aside lesson content. Rather, we will expand the scope of what we would normally consider academic content beyond mere facts, concepts, and skills by adding metacognition, relevance, and communication.
2. Thinking skill—the world needs solid, flexible thinkers. Students of history not only need to remember and understand the causes of the Civil War, they must be able to analyze and evaluate them. Students of English language arts need to not only remember the rules of grammar but also how to apply them to create their own contributions. Much like mechanics

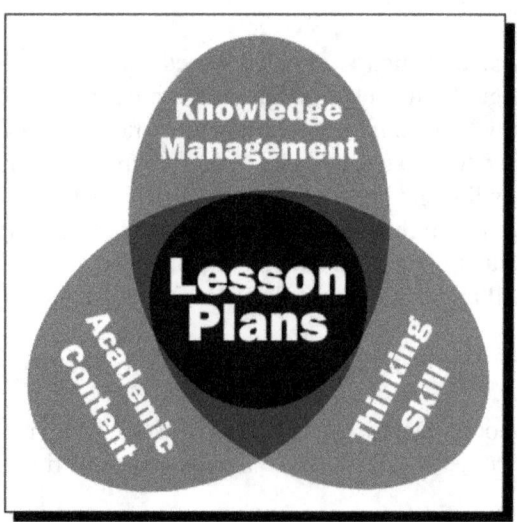

Figure I.1 The Superposition of Academic Content, Thinking Skills, and Knowledge Management Embodies the Essence of Rigorous Instruction. *Source*: Author.

need to purchase a large assortment of wrenches, students also need to accumulate a wide range of cognitive skills.
3. Knowledge management—future careers will increase demands on an employee's ability to accumulate information from numerous sources, filter important information from minutiae, make informed decisions, and communicate results. Increased skill in knowledge management allows one to assume larger loads of responsibility and lead others in moving forward. In short, knowledge management helps students rise in an organization's structure once they enter the workforce.

This book directly maps each of these lesson goals to each of three classification schemes denoted as Depth of Knowledge (DOK), Knowledge Dimension (KD), and the Cognitive Process Dimension (CPD). We will describe each scheme shortly.

Lesson Goals		Dimension
Academic Content	⇔	Knowledge Dimension (KD)
Thinking Skill	⇔	Cognitive Process Dimension (CPD)
Knowledge Management	⇔	Depth of Knowledge (DOK)

What's missing in our understanding of lesson content? Some will point to socio-emotional learning while others will call for character development. However, many of these issues point to a teacher's own priorities and teaching style. Nothing in this book will prevent teachers from layering their lesson plans with such skills. Rather, this book focuses on the fundamentals that can drive any lesson plan, no matter the teacher or subject.

WHAT IS RIGOR?

Much has been made in education of the etymology of the word "rigor." Use of this word in education first started appearing in the 1990s with the rise of state content standards and standardized testing. Because of this close tie to such controversial issues, the word "rigor" soon became associated with a heartless, rigid, and emotionless view of education. Opponents of rigor pointed out uses of the word "rigor" in *rigor mortis* and asked "Do you want your instruction to be stiff and cold?"

The word "rigor," however, also has a basis in science, which likely forms the origin of the term as it is used in education. A rigorous experiment is one in which scientists choose no shortcuts to producing meaningful work that accurately reflects reality. Southern Cross University offers a description of rigor that is particularly apt:

Intellectual rigour is having clarity in thinking and an ability to think carefully, deeply and with rigour when faced with new knowledge and arguments. This capability involves engaging constructively and methodically when exploring ideas, theories and philosophies. It also relates to the ability to analyse and construct knowledge with depth, insight and intellectual maturity. A student develops this attribute as part of the challenge of ongoing and systematic study. Intellectual rigour is encouraged for example during an assessment exercise where a debate or discussion occurs about a challenging topic. The challenge for the student is to have the ability to consider other points of view and make a thoughtful argument. (Southern Cross University n.d.)

Rigor, or intellectual rigor as Southern Cross University calls it, is about bending over backward in a cognitive sense to understand content from a wide range of angles. As Wagner explains: "Rigor for the 21st century includes a focus on skills for life: critical thinking and problem solving, collaboration and leadership, agility and adaptability, initiative and entrepreneurialism, effective oral and written communication, accessing and analyzing information, and curiosity and imagination" (Wagner 2008, Blackburn and Williamson 2009). That doesn't sound like rigor mortis at all.

In short, rigorous instruction compels students to leave no stone unturned in their quest to learn content. Table I.1 provides more impressions of how

Table I.1 Definitions of Rigor, as Compiled by Blackburn and Williamson. (Blackburn and Williamson, 2009)

Source	Description
Bogess (2007)	Quality of thinking, not quantity, can occur in any grade and at any subject
Wasley, Hampel, and Clark (1997)	High expectations are important and must include effort on the part of the learner
Washor and Mojkowki (2006)	Deep immersion in a subject which should include real-world settings and working with an expert
Beane (2001)	Rigor would be used to say something about how an experience or activity is carried out and to what degree. Specifically, a "rigorous" experience would be one that involves depth and care as, for example, in a scientific experiment or literary analysis that is done thoughtfully, deeply with sufficient depth and attention to accuracy and detail
Strong, Silver and Perrini (2001)	Goal of helping students develop the capacity to understand content that is complex, ambiguous, provocative, and personally or emotionally challenging
Wagner (2008)	Rigor for the twenty-first century includes a focus on skills for life: critical thinking and problem solving, collaboration and leadership, agility and adaptability, initiative and entrepreneurialism, effective oral and written communication, accessing and analyzing information, and curiosity and imagination

the word "rigor" is used as collected from various sources (Blackburn and Williamson 2009). Such interpretations of rigor (and not rigor mortis) will guide our discussion from this point forward.

TERMINOLOGY

The education field has fewer standards of terminology and nomenclature than (say) physics, law, or medicine. Because definitions often change markedly over time, confusion often swamps meaningful discussion. Before embarking any further, we should clarify some terms that we will encounter throughout this book.

- The term "Bloom's Taxonomy" often refers to both the original taxonomy of 1956 (Bloom et al. 1956) and the revised taxonomy of 2001 (Anderson et al. 2001, Krathwohl 2002). This book relies far more heavily on the revised taxonomy. For the sake of brevity, Bloom's Taxonomy in this book refers to the revised taxonomy unless stated otherwise.
- By the same token, many educators equate the term "Bloom's Taxonomy" only with its CPD, disregarding the KD altogether. Because lesson planning in this book leans so heavily on the use of both, we will refer to the CPD and Bloom's Taxonomy separately.
- We will abbreviate the Cognitive Process Dimension as CPD and the Knowledge Dimension as KD for brevity.
- Many educators refer to the six categories of the CPD as *levels*. However, Anderson and Krathwohl referred to them as *categories* (Anderson et al. 2001, Krathwohl 2002). Likewise, we will use the term "categories."

DEPTH OF KNOWLEDGE (DOK)

Once developed by Norman Webb, Depth of Knowledge (DOK) represented the biggest step in understanding curriculum since 1956, the year Bloom's Taxonomy was unveiled. Although DOK now appears in countless trainings across the nation, much of the focus centers on selecting the proper level of sample problems. Rather, we will use DOK to create culminating activities for our lessons, as well as offer guidelines on delivering questions to students during instruction.

The four levels of DOK itemized in table I.2 characterize different ways students can interact with content, beginning with the least cognitive demand, DOK-1, and increasing to the highest cognitive complexity, DOK-4.

DOK does not measure the difficulty of content. For example, a DOK-1 question could ask students to recite a short limerick or a complete speech.

Table I.2 Webb's Depth-of-Knowledge (DOK) Levels, Where DOK-1 Refers to Level 1 of Depth of Knowledge, and So On. (Webb 1999, Webb 2002, Webb 2005, Hess et al. 2009)

Level	Description
DOK-1	*Recall and Reproduction*—recall a fact, term, principle, or concept; perform a routine procedure.
DOK-2	*Basic Application of Skills/Concepts*—use information, conceptual knowledge; select appropriate procedures for a task; perform two or more steps with decision points along the way; solve routine problems; organize or display data; interpret or use simple graphs.
DOK-3	*Strategic Thinking*—reason or develop a plan to approach a problem; employ some decision-making and justification; solve abstract, complex, or non-routine problems, complex. (DOK-3 problems often allow more than one possible answer.)
DOK-4	*Extended Thinking*—perform investigations or apply concepts/skills to the real world that require time to research, problem solve, and process multiple conditions of the problem or task; perform non-routine manipulations across disciplines, content areas, or multiple sources.

The same can be said for computing the expression $(12.4)^3$, which is no more rigorous than computing $(12)^3$ or even 2^3. Therefore, simplifying content by using smaller numbers or using passages with simpler vocabulary rarely lowers the DOK of the activity.

Conversely, students must dig deeper into their understanding to explain how or why something works (DOK-2), apply it to real-world phenomena with justification and supporting evidence (DOK-3), or integrate one concept with other concepts or other perspectives (DOK-4) to produce novel ideas or solutions (Hess 2009, Hess et al. 2009).

DOK descriptors provide content-specific examples that illustrate how students might move toward deeper understanding with more complex or abstract content (Hess 2009, Hess et al. 2009). Identifying the DOK levels of questions in tests or class assignments can help teachers articulate how deeply students must understand the related content to complete the necessary tasks. (A feature of DOK we will avail greatly in chapter 1.)

We can also describe DOK in terms of the knowledge management needed to complete a task. For example, the amount of researching, discussion, decision-making, and information disaggregation/aggregation students must employ is substantially higher when students need to determine whether a certain war was a Civil War (which would likely reside at the DOK-2 or DOK-3 levels), then to identify the major battles of the war (which resides at only the DOK-1 level).

DOK levels therefore form another important perspective of cognitive complexity. In this scheme, the complexity of both the content (e.g., simple vs. complex data displays; interpreting literal vs. figurative language) and the task required (e.g., solving routine vs. nonroutine problems) determine this cognitive demand. In short, the four DOK levels identify four different and deeper ways a student might interact with content.

Interpreting and assigning intended DOK levels to both the standards and the related assessment items are now essential requirements in any alignment analyses. These levels have been applied across all content areas and many states and districts use DOK to designate the depth and complexity of state standards so as to align the state's large-scale assessments or to revise existing standards to achieve higher cognitive levels for instruction (Hess et al. 2009). Consequently, teachers need to develop the ability to design instruction and create units of study/curriculum and classroom assessments for a greater range of cognitive demand (The Standards Company 2008, Hess et al. 2009).

COGNITIVE PROCESS DIMENSION (CPD) OF BLOOM'S TAXONOMY

The CPD of Bloom's Taxonomy shown in table I.3 has experienced wide deployment, including its use in education technology (e.g., Bloom's Digital Taxonomy (TeachThought 2018)) and neuroscience research (Kaufer 2011). On the more pedagogical side, the CPD can help teachers analyze their curriculum, instruction, and assessment, as well as develop lesson questions. Although later revised by a team of education researchers headed by Anderson and Krathwohl, the overall intent of the Taxonomy remains: *Categorize questions and activities according to their type of cognition* (Anderson et al. 2001).

We will use the CPD to select appropriate teaching methods for delivering the lesson content to develop rich, stimulating questions to stir engagement and check for understanding. Each category is associated with an action verb that, in most but not all circumstances, typifies the Bloom's Taxonomy category.

Confusion between DOK and the CPD

The arrival of DOK as a perceived rival to the CPD of Bloom's Taxonomy meant that it would not be long before educators began confusing the two schemas. Some of the confusion manifested into misleading charts and tables that surfaced in early trainings that still persist today. These grew out of crude attempts to map the familiar six categories of the CPD into the four levels of DOK, therefore, creating a shortcut to understanding the new rigor measure.

The unfortunate example in figure I.2 attempts to align each of the four levels of DOK to certain action verbs associated with classroom assignments.

Table I.3 The Cognitive Process Dimension of Bloom's Taxonomy and Sample Action Verbs. (Anderson et al. 2001)

Category	Description	Example verbs
Remember	Retrieve relevant knowledge from long-term memory	recognize, recall
Understand	Construct meaning from instructional messages, including oral, written, and graphic communication	explain, summarize, infer, classify, compare
Apply	Carry out or use a procedure in a given situation	execute, implement
Analyze	Break material into its constituent parts and determine how the parts relate to one another and to an overall structure or purpose	differentiate, organize, attribute
Evaluate	Make judgments based on criteria and standards	check, critique
Create	Put elements together to form a coherent or functional whole; reorganize elements into a new pattern or structure	generate, plan, produce

The DOK Wheel bases its design on the fundamental, but false, premise that we can simply select certain action verbs to raise and lower the DOK level of instruction.

As one example, the action verb "design" appears in the DOK-4 section of the DOK Wheel Chart. However, a teacher asking students to design an engineering apparatus is not assigning a DOK-4 activity unless she prompts her students to employ mathematical or scientific principles into their design. And although the verb "calculate" appears in the DOK-1 section of the wheel chart, any student of mathematics knows that calculations can reach up far into DOK-4.

Unfortunately, the DOK Wheel Chart appears in countless trainings throughout the country. Norman Webb is often asked for permission to use the chart in the mistaken belief that he created it. To the contrary, he considers the wheel chart misleading and has always discouraged its use. As he puts it, "The only possible use of the chart I can see is if someone took a verb and asked how it could be placed in each of the four sectors."[1]

Karin Hess, probably the most prolific national trainer on DOK, has also weighed in on the DOK Wheel Chart.

> I call this the "DOK wheel of misfortune" and tell people in my workshops to discard it. It flies in the face of what DOK is about: What comes *after* the verb. I usually point out that, for example, comparing two story characters (DOK 2) does not show as deep understanding as comparing (analyzing across

Introduction

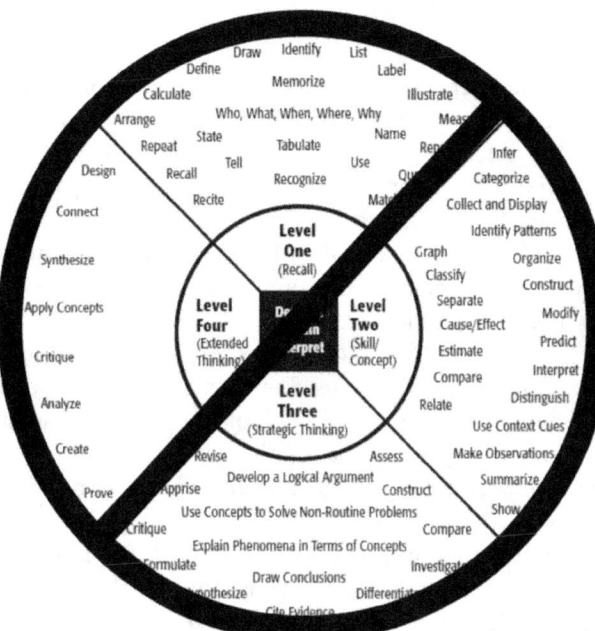

Figure I.2 The Pervasive DOK Wheel Tries to Associate the Action Verbs Associated with Bloom's Taxonomy to the Four Depth of Knowledge Levels. Unfortunately, it is incorrect. (The red circle/slash was added to discourage replication.) *Source*: Author.

texts) themes from two different stories (DOK 4). Secondly, verbs alone are "generic" to content and again research tells us that analyzing in science, for example, does not require the same mental schemas as analyzing literature or mathematics.[2]

Because of the confusion between DOK and CPD, it is wise to take a moment to distinguish between these two classification schemes. We will begin with DOK.

Consider the tasks assigned to the traditional soldier engaged in a battle that occurred in (say) World War I. Although privates at that time would have employed a full range of the CPD during the course of their operations, almost all of these tasks would have resided at the most straightforward level of complexity.

In other words, while soldiers at that time would have needed to evaluate their own battlefield situations according to criteria they learned in training, the amount of information and cognitive processing needed to do so would have been relatively modest. Rarely would privates have needed lengthy discussion to perform such evaluations. In this sense, we can say that privates in the distant past carried out tasks mostly associated with DOK-1 and DOK-2.

On the other hand, generals at that time (and today) would have needed to process a vast array of information on the enemy and their own prior knowledge to formulate effective strategies and campaigns. Strategic discussions would have been often long and involved input from multiple parties. In this sense, we can say that generals performed more cognitively complex tasks associated with the DOK-3 and DOK-4 levels. So, it appears that traditional soldiers of yore would have encountered situations demanding increasing DOK as they rose through the ranks.

Today, the modern military is casting aside this highly siloed model of military leadership for good reasons. For one, the demands of technology require considerably more complex cognition on the part of soldiers than in the past. More importantly, the modern military now understands that soldiers who have the mental flexibility to meet challenging tasks are more effective in battle.

DOK can therefore serve as a powerful vehicle for leadership training related to all forms of organizational management. (Business schools take note.) As such, DOK can be likened to *knowledge management*; the higher the DOK, the more knowledge management needed to process the activity prompt (such as a question) and formulate a quality response.

On the flip side, we can liken the CDP of Bloom's Taxonomy as a means of describing the *type of thinking* that one must engage to respond to a question or perform an activity. In this sense, the CDP is highly neurological, as described by Daniela Kaufer of the University of California:

> Cognitive functions associated with the lower levels [categories] of Bloom's Taxonomy, such as understanding and remembering, are associated with the hippocampus (the area of the brain responsible for memory and spatial awareness). The higher-level cognitive functions of Bloom's Taxonomy, such as creating, evaluating, analyzing, and applying, involve the cortical areas responsible for decision-making, association, and motivation. More complex thought processes are more beneficial for learning because they involve a greater number of neural connections and more neurological cross-talk. (Kaufer 2011)

Kaufer goes on to say something important for teachers (and the military) to remember:

> Active learning takes advantage of this cross-talk, stimulating a variety of areas of the brain and promoting memory. (Kaufer 2011)

In short, the CPD of Bloom's Taxonomy offers a practical way to improve cognitive skill akin to exercising the brain. By asking students to answer questions that span a wide range of the CPD, teachers are in essence strengthening a wider array of neural networks.

Unlike DOK, where each level describes how deeply students engage with the content of a lesson, the CPD can be typified by the type of thinking used to formulate responses. These types of thinking can be mapped to a reasonable extent to certain action verbs.

Let us refer back to our military analogy. During field operations, foot soldiers need to *remember* and *understand* important information they learned in boot camp, *apply* their knowledge to new situations they encounter on the battlefield, *analyze* the behavior of the enemy, and *evaluate* their own situation with respect to established criteria. In certain circumstances, they may need to *create* novel solutions to challenges they encounter during their operations. Each verb points to a distinct form of cognition. In this regard, the neurological demand of a well-trained private is similar to that of a general, who also exhibits the full range of Bloom's Taxonomy when carrying out duties.

ENTER COGNITIVE RIGOR

Cognitive Rigor is a two-dimensional classification scheme for establishing the cognitive demand of questions and tasks. The associated Cognitive Rigor Matrix comprises two axes: DOK along Axis 1 and the CPD of Bloom's Taxonomy along Axis 2, as shown in figure I.3.

The Cognitive Rigor Matrix is commonly used to assess curricular quality since its development in 2005 (Lane 2010, SBAC 2015, NWEA 2016, WeLearnNYC, n.d.). However, we will employ the matrix as a lesson *design* tool and not just to classify the cognitive demand of tasks and questions.

The matrix allows educators to uniquely categorize and examine selected assignments/learning activities assigned to students (Hess et al. 2009, Weldon 2016, Carlson 2017, Karuguti et al. 2017, Shive 2017). For example, the rote completion of simple mathematical routines, often derided by the moniker "plug and chug," targets the (DOK-1, Bloom-3/Apply) cell of the matrix. Figure I.4 shows a simple 2×2 portion of the matrix with verb examples drawn from math and science activities.

KNOWLEDGE DIMENSION OF BLOOM'S TAXONOMY

We will add a third dimension to the Cognitive Rigor Matrix—an expanded form of the KD of Bloom's Taxonomy. The KD is often overlooked because of

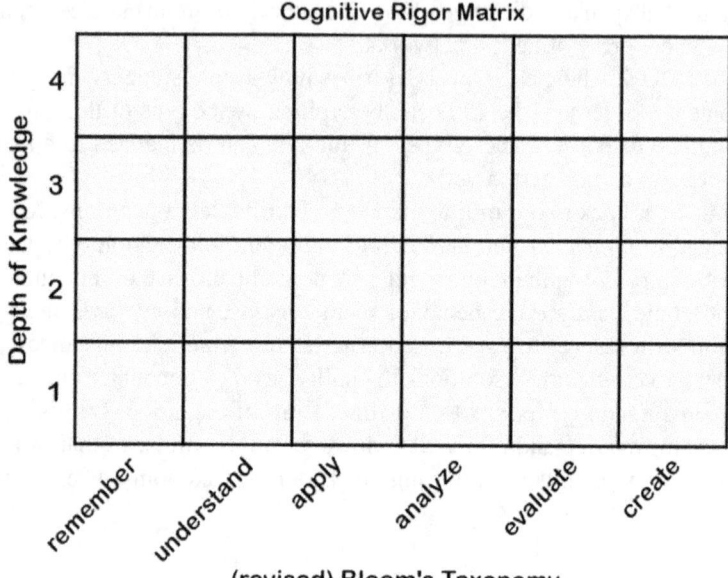

Figure I.3 The Cognitive Rigor Matrix Designed for Large-Scale Education Research Projects (The Standards Company LLC 2008, Hess et al. 2009). *Source*: Author.

	DOK-1	DOK-2
Understand	Evaluate an expression Locate points on a grid or number on a number line Solve a one-step problem Represent math relationships in words, pictures, or symbols Read, write, compare decimals in scientific notation	Specify and explain relationships Explain steps followed Summarize results or concepts Make basic inferences or logical predictions from data/observations Use models /diagrams to represent or explain mathematical concepts Make and explain estimates
Apply	Follow recipe-type procedures Calculate, measure, apply a rule Apply algorithm or formula Solve linear equations Convert among representations or numbers, or within and between customary and metric measures	Solve routine problem applying multiple concepts or decision points Retrieve information from a table, graph, or figure and use it solve a multi-step problem Translate between tables, graphs, words, and symbolic notations Construct models given criteria

Figure I.4 Four Sample Cells of the Cognitive Rigor Matrix for Math and Science Instruction Completed by Hess (2014). According to the Matrix, evaluating a mathematical expression requires less knowledge management (Measured by DOK) and a substantially different type of thinking (categorized by Bloom's taxonomy) than selecting a procedure according to criteria and performing it. *Source*: Author.

the notoriety of its sibling, the CPD. Despite its low visibility, the KD serves an important role in lesson planning, that is, establishing the content of the lesson.

The original KD comprised four components: (1) factual knowledge, (2) conceptual knowledge, (3) procedural knowledge, and (4) metacognitive knowledge which are described as follows: (Anderson et al. 2011, Krathwohl 2002)

- Factual knowledge refers to the basic elements a student must know to be acquainted with a discipline or solve problems in it.
- Conceptual knowledge refers to the interrelationships among the basic elements within a larger structure that enable them to function together.
- Procedural knowledge refers to how to *do* something, methods of inquiry, and criteria for using skills, algorithms, techniques, and methods.
- Metacognitive knowledge is awareness and knowledge of one's own cognition and about oneself in relation to various subject matters.

These four levels are shown in table I.4. The lesson planning approach in this book supplements the original list with two categories of its own: (1) relevance knowledge and (2) communicative knowledge. Technically speaking, both were included in various components of the original KD. Separating them out, however, helps ensure that these critical features of learning are not overlooked.

- Relevance knowledge refers to students understanding *why* they are being asked to learn the lesson.
- Communicative knowledge addresses vocabulary development beyond merely knowing the definition of words but also includes presentation skills, writing skills, and collaboration.

In summary, the expanded KD used in this book comprises six dimensions: (1) factual knowledge, (2) conceptual knowledge, (3) procedural knowledge,

Table I.4 The Four Components of the Knowledge Dimension Devised by Anderson and Krathwohl. (Anderson et al. 2001, Krathwohl 2002)

Factual	Conceptual	Procedural	Metacognitive
Knowledge of terminology	Knowledge of classifications and categories	Knowledge of subject-specific skills and algorithms	Strategic knowledge
Knowledge of specific details and elements	Knowledge of principles and generalizations	Knowledge of subject-specific techniques and methods	Knowledge about cognitive tasks, including appropriate contextual and conditional knowledge
	Knowledge of theories, models, and structures	Knowledge of criteria for determining when to use appropriate procedures	Self-knowledge

(4) metacognitive knowledge, (5) relevance knowledge, and (6) communicative knowledge.

From this point on, the term "KD" will refer to these six components. An important step in lesson planning is deciding what constitutes the KD for the topic at hand.

THE TAXONOMY TABLE

The Taxonomy Table developed by Anderson and Krathwohl is an educational tool used to interpret how students process different types of knowledge (Anderson et al. 2001, Krathwohl 2002). Like the Cognitive Rigor Matrix, the Taxonomy Table comprises two axes: the KD along one axis and the CPD along the other axis.

The Taxonomy Table has been used by educators to assess curriculum and develop large overlying lesson plans since its publication. However, the role that this tool plays in this book is somewhat different—we will use this superposition of the KD and the CDP to align the content in our lesson plans to teaching strategies deemed capable of delivering the content in the classroom.

THE RIGOR CUBE

While the Cognitive Rigor Matrix is a valuable tool for assessing the rigor of curriculum and instruction, adding a third dimension to the matrix helps identify the content of lessons for lesson planning purposes. This third axis will be based on the expanded KD; this added dimension extends the existing Cognitive Rigor Matrix to the three-dimensional model shown in figure I.5, with each dimension playing distinctive roles in lesson planning.

This new model, called the Rigor Cube, forms the framework for developing lesson plans throughout this book. As can be seen, one face of the Rigor Cube is the Cognitive Rigor Matrix and another face is the Taxonomy Table. (The third face, which superposes DOK and the expanded KD, has no obvious utility.)

Naturally, we want to avoid creating lessons that fail to provide students with cognitively challenging learning. Luckily, each of the three axes of the Rigor Cube in table I.5 provides a safeguard against thin, low-level lesson plans. In short, we will use the DOK and KD axes to plan our lessons. Then, we will use the CPD axis to set up strategies for delivering the lesson to students. Finally, we will use both the DOK and CDP axes to develop formative assessments for our lessons.

Introduction xxxi

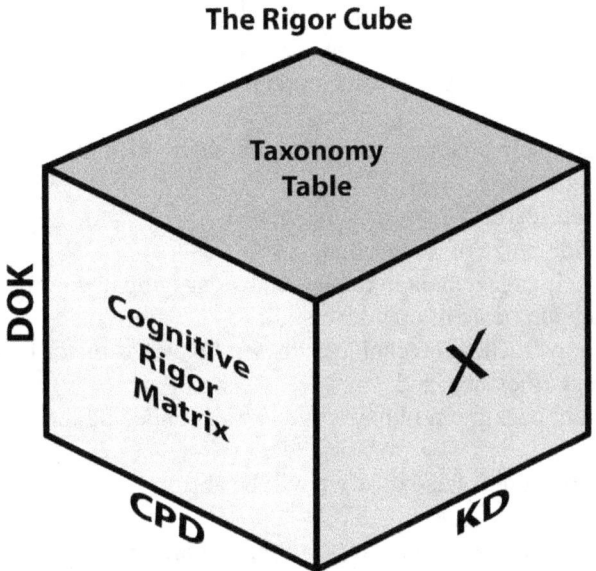

Figure I.5 The Rigor Cube Supplements the Original Cognitive Rigor Matrix (The Standards Company LLC 2008, Hess et al. 2009) with a Third Axis, the Knowledge Dimension (KD) of Bloom's Taxonomy (California Department of Education 2014). The upper surface represents the taxonomy table found in the revised Bloom's taxonomy book by Anderson and Krathwohl. The superposition of DOK and KD has no known applications. All three axes of the Rigor Cube play distinctive roles in lesson planning. *Source:* Author.

Table I.5 The Three Axes of the Rigor Cube and Their Role in Developing Rigorous Lesson Planning.

Axis	Purpose
Depth of Knowledge (DOK)	Match the depth of learning in the culminating activity to expectations.
	Guide effective questioning techniques.
Cognitive Process Dimension (CPD)	Select effective instructional strategies to deliver the lesson contents.
	Create engaging questions that probe a wide range of intellect.
Knowledge Dimension (KD)	Identify the content of the lesson.

WHAT DO WE WANT TO ACHIEVE?

Until now, no one has created a clear path toward coalescing the power of DOK and the two dimensions of Bloom's Taxonomy to drive pedagogy, from lesson planning to post-instruction assessment. We will change all that.

Let us first outline a few goals that will help our students achieve the college/career-preparedness skills that form the focus of so much education reform. More specifically, we want students to

- demonstrate their attainment of a certain DOK of the subject through a culminating activity,
- connect their learning to other subject areas,
- obtain a wide range of knowledge,
- heighten their engagement in the lesson by engaging in vigorous discourse,
- exercise a wide range of cognitive skill,
- experience instructional techniques chosen by the instructor for their effectiveness and efficiency, and
- learn without background-knowledge barriers impeding their progress.

Upon completion of this book, we will be able to

- understand, compare, and contrast all three dimensions of the Rigor Cube, that is, the CPD of Bloom's Revised Taxonomy, the KD of Bloom's Revised Taxonomy, and the DOK,
- analyze curricular materials with respect to each Rigor Cube axis,
- apply the Rigor Cube to create rigorous lesson plans aligned to new college/career-readiness standards, and
- use the Rigor Cube to evaluate classroom instruction with respect to school-wide goals for improving student learning.

Table I.6 summarizes the steps used in developing lesson plans. We will follow the flow chart in figure I.6, where chapter 1 will address Step 1—establishing the scope of the lesson by selecting the state standard and topic we wish to address and identifying a career focus to widen the reach of the lesson.

Step 2 in chapter 2 leverages the first axis of the Rigor Cube, DOK, to create a culminating activity for the lesson. We will avail the manner in which the DOK can match the goal of the lesson with our expectations of student success. We will also establish learning objectives and language objectives for our lesson plans.

Step 3 in chapter 3 leverages the second axis of the Rigor Cube—the KD of Bloom's Taxonomy—to establish the content of the lesson and define proficiency. This content will not only encompass the grade-level concepts/skills we expect students to learn, but will also address the background knowledge that we expect them to already possess (but for which they might not).

Step 4 in chapter 4 uses the third axis of the Rigor Cube—the CPD of Bloom's Taxonomy—to select instructional techniques from the myriad at our disposal. Chapter 5 also addresses Step 4, focusing on techniques for

Introduction

Table I.6 The Five Steps of Lesson Planning. Here, DOK, KD, and CPD Stand for Depth of Knowledge, the expanded Knowledge Dimension of Bloom's Taxonomy, and the Cognitive Process Dimension of Bloom's Taxonomy, Respectively.

Step	Chapter	Label	Axis	Description
1	1	Lesson Scope	—	Select a standard and topic to meet guidelines for standards-based instruction, then choose a cross-disciplinary focus to broaden horizons.
2	2	Knowledge Management	DOK	Craft a culminating activity that allows students to demonstrate what they learned in the lesson.
3	3	Lesson Content	KD	Identify the facts, concepts, skills, metacognition, relevance, and communicative skills students need to learn to complete the culminating activity.
4	4	Instructional Strategies	CPD	Identify promising teaching strategies that can deliver the lesson content to students.
5	5	Background Barriers	CPD	Provide subskill scaffolding to help students acquire needed background knowledge.
5	6	Assessment	DOK/CPD	Establish questions and tasks to engage students and check for understanding.

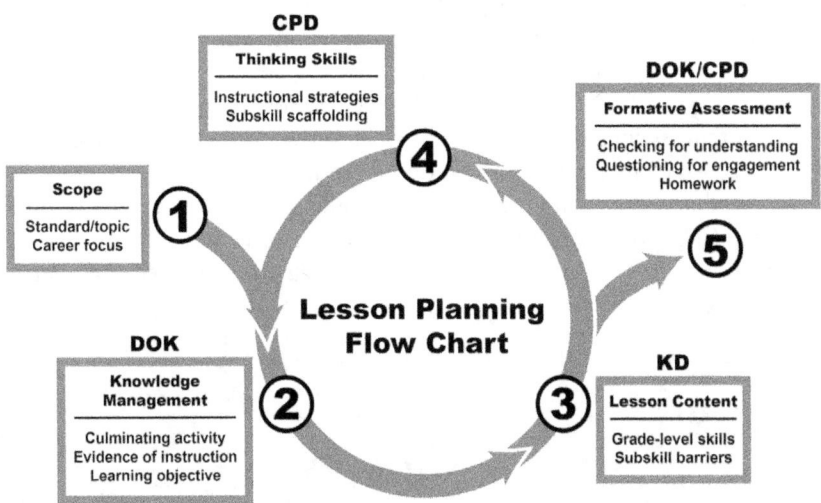

Figure I.6 Flow Chart Used for Developing Effective Lesson Plans. Chapters 1 to 6 will address each step of the lesson planning process. *Source*: Author.

overcoming students' lack of background knowledge. As shown in figure I.6, once finished with Step 4, we can pass through Steps 2–4 if necessary to adjust our lesson expectations, adjust the lesson content, or select new instructional methods.

Once we have tightened Steps 2–4 to our liking, we will advance to Step 5 of the lesson planning process in chapter 6, where we will establish formative assessment strategies for the lesson. We will distinguish checking for understanding and questioning for engagement and learn a mnemonic device for questioning students. In chapter 7, we will provide a slice-of-life example of a career-technical education teacher preparing her lesson plan from scratch, illustrating her thought processes and decision-making as she passes through each step of the lesson planning flowchart.

Before moving on to the next chapter, let us address some questions that may have already surfaced in your mind.

1. Will the Rigor Cube work with a specific teaching method, like the Socratic method? Absolutely. In fact, the selection of a teaching method to deliver the content is a distinct step in this approach.
2. Can I develop PBL lessons with the Rigor Cube? Because each lesson begins with a culminating activity that guides student learning toward a clear goal, the Rigor Cube is ideally suited for PBL.
3. What about direct instruction? The Rigor Cube can incorporate direct instruction effortlessly. In fact, all five sample lessons in this book incorporate direct instruction to teach sizable portions of the content.
4. How hard is it to use the Rigor Cube? The approach used in this book is relatively straightforward and systematic. Developing quality lesson plans should pose no barrier to any teacher.
5. What if I teach elementary school? The examples used in this book are specific to secondary school teachers but any teacher can use the Rigor Cube. (An elementary school edition is forthcoming.)
6. What if I teach a non-core subject like auto shop? Teachers can use the Rigor Cube to teach any academic topic. In fact, the Rigor Cube is no harder to apply to career-technical education than any other academic subjects.

So, let's begin!

NOTES

1. Personal correspondence. December 13, 2014 (email).
2. Personal correspondence. December 27, 2013 (email).

Chapter 1

Lesson Scope

It would have been nice to dive right into lesson planning in this chapter. But our approach to instruction relies on understanding the building blocks of lesson planning. As a result, we have centered our discussion so far on DOK, the two Bloom's Taxonomy classification schemes, and how they combine to form the Rigor Cube. But lesson planning and delivery is where the "rubber meets the road." Somehow theory must flow into practice, lest the Rigor Cube becomes little more than a talking point for coffee-shop arguments.

At this point, our lesson planning begins. We will refer to the flowchart discussed in the previous chapter. As we can see from Step 1 in figure 1.1, our lesson planning starts out like most methods by compelling us to outline the chosen standards and topics. However, this process features a twist: we will consider embedding a career focus into the lesson scope at the outset. In short, we will address three questions in particular:

1. Which primary standard do we want to address?
2. Which topic of this standard will we focus on for the lesson at hand?
3. Which cross-disciplinary focus will we use to supplement our lesson?

STATE CONTENT STANDARDS AND TOPICS

Love it or hate it, standards-based instruction is a fact of life. That said, our approach will remain agnostic as far as our choice of standards is concerned. But we still want to deliver a standards-based lesson. Therefore, selecting a primary standard is a logical first step.

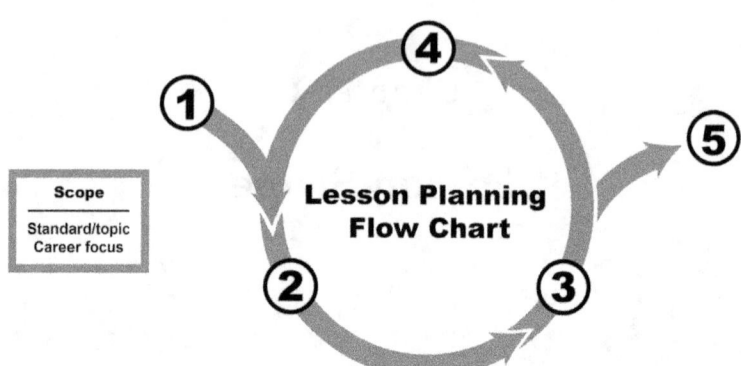

Figure 1.1   This Chapter Focuses on Step 1 of the Lesson Planning Flow Chart, Where We Establish the Scope of the Lesson. *Source*: Author.

Choosing a Standard

The movement toward a national adoption for state content standards is important for a number of reasons. For one, students who mastered grade-level work in one school could reasonably expect to be prepared for the next grade level at another school, even if they travel across state lines. Furthermore, national standards ensured that schools were not sabotaging the rigor of curriculum and instruction in an effort to pass students through the system.

The state-led effort to develop the Common Core State Standards (CCSS) was launched in 2009 by state leaders, including governors and state commissioners of education from forty-eight states, two territories and the District of Columbia, through their membership in the National Governors Association and the Council of Chief State School Officers (CCSSO).

After their introduction, the CCSS polarized education like no other issue in history, although the resistance to their use in the classroom has somewhat abated. Resistance exploded once Arne Duncan, the U.S. Secretary of Education under President Barack Obama, mandated their adoption for states pursuing lucrative federal funding, therefore giving the false impression that the CCSS was federal in origin. Conspiracy theories centered on a federal takeover of public education ensued. Poorly conceived lesson plans designed to meet the Common Core went viral, adding to the ridicule. The CCSS has survived the attacks, however. Today, all but nine states have adopted them.

The Next Generation Science Standards (NGSS) was a multistate effort to help students understand core scientific concepts, acquire scientific concepts and skills that transcend a wide range of standards, and learn the science and engineering process. The NGSS has seen less widespread adoption than the CCSS. There was little financial reason to do so; adoption processes are expensive for both the state and its schools, but the federal government never provided such funding. Furthermore, many states balked at what they considered some of the more controversial topics in the NGSS such as evolution, climate change, and the age of the Earth.

The Common Core and NGSS address core subjects; therefore, much of the professional development teachers receive centers on instruction related to these national standards. However, teachers in noncore subjects are still compelled to teach standards-based lessons. In consideration of their needs, the lesson planning process described in this book includes examples from noncore subjects.

Rather than focus on just math or English language arts, this lesson planning process is designed to be robust and, therefore, applicable to a wide range of subjects. For the sake of brevity, we will need to settle on relatively few example standards, for which we will develop sample lesson plans side by side for the remainder of this book. One lesson will target a middle school English language arts standard selected from the CCSS. Another lesson will focus on the Common Core math standards. We will follow this lesson with a high school STEM lesson aligned to the NGSS.

Finally, a lot of professional development materials leave noncore standards out of the discussion. We will not make this mistake. The CTE field reflects by far the widest range of subjects in all of K-12 instruction. One of our sample lessons will center on teaching a high school art standard. Our final sample lesson, which is developed as a vignette in chapter 7, will focus on criminal justice and will be guided by the Nevada CTE standards.

Choosing a Topic

Once we have identified a standard, we need to choose a topic for the lesson. The act of choosing a topic is greatly aided by unpacking the standard, for which we will follow a systematic approach.

Our first step when reading a standard is to identify key concepts and skills (what should they know?) and their learning targets (what do they need to understand?). One way to accomplish this is to read the standard and identify the nouns (concepts) and verbs (skills) and mark them appropriately. We should also mark the context, which places constraints on the standard. Such context is nearly always expressed as a prepositional phrase. In this book, we will mark the concepts and skills with brackets < > and { }, respectively. We will use square brackets [ ] for the context.

The act of choosing a topic, therefore, amounts to selecting a narrower combination of concepts and skills while remaining true to the context of the standard. Naturally, we may want to recast the language somewhat, all the while remaining faithful to the spirit of the standard. For example, consider the following CCSS standard (Common Core State Standards Initiative 2010):

Use verbs in the active and passive voice and in the conditional and subjunctive mood to achieve particular effects (e.g., emphasizing the actor or the action; expressing uncertainty or describing a state contrary to fact).

Using our convention, we can identify the various parts of the standard:

{Use} ⟨verbs⟩ [in the active and passive voice] and [in the conditional and subjunctive mood] to {achieve} ⟨particular effects (e.g., emphasizing the actor or the action; expressing uncertainty or describing a state contrary to fact)⟩.

That portion of the standard in parentheses is the only suggested vehicle to meet the standard. Selecting a smaller combination of nouns, verbs, and context, we obtain the following unpacked standard:

{Use} ⟨verbs⟩ [in the active and passive voice] to {achieve} ⟨ emphasize the actor or the action⟩

The working standard for the lesson could therefore be:

Use verbs in the active and passive voice to emphasize the actor or the action.

Students who can use the active voice to emphasize the actor in a sentence will therefore meet the procedural knowledge related to this standard. There is a lot more to meeting standards of proficiency for this standard, however. Such additional demands are addressed using the expanded Knowledge Dimension (KD) in Step 3 of the lesson planning process described in chapter 3.

CHOOSING A CAREER FOCUS

Real-world context compels students to take a stronger interest in the lesson and creates a tighter link between academic lessons and their personal desires. But traditional lessons often shoehorn one topic into another for which no real connection exists, producing a contrived career focus. What is the point of asking students to calculate the kinetic energy of a dancer during a visual arts lesson? By the same token, does writing math-themed limericks serve any real purpose? Lesson planning should strive to promote *real* connections among disciplines.

Daily instruction should feature a broad range of subjects. While teachers often rely on the four core subjects as potential targets for cross-disciplinary instruction, myriad other possibilities appear. Business principles pose as useful targets because they strongly tie to career preparedness and because K-12 students rarely receive formal instruction in this area. By incorporating a business focus into lesson plans, we can teach students that they will need to not only have an interest in this field but will also need to understand basic business practices to thrive.

The government sector provides another career focus, as does the field of engineering, especially for math and science lessons. Medicine, technical writing, and marketing offer even more possibilities.

What about those students who have no interest in the chosen career focus? It would be easy to allow students to choose a different career focus if so desired. This is one way that teachers can differentiate instruction. However, there is an argument for assigning all students the same career focus. Lesson plans not only guide the teaching of academic content, they can also broaden a student's horizon. Many students have no desire to be a quality control engineer or a policy advisor because they know little about these fields. But a student who has no interest in city government while in middle school might be a city manager someday. Today's sports journalist might have wanted to be a biologist in high school. Sometimes lessons need to coax students out of their comfort zones to expose them to what life has to offer.

Service Providers

Sometime during the 1980s, education shifted away from job skills and toward college preparedness. Auto shop and welding classes all but disappeared, to be replaced by Advanced Placement courses. This left behind many students who had little interest in college but could have enjoyed rewarding careers nonetheless. Since then, the pendulum has shifted back to much extent. Today, career tech education (CTE) is taken more seriously.

Some of these CTE programs target careers that are high in demand and pay solid wages, often higher than careers that require college degrees. Anyone that has had a mechanic work on their car knows that their fees can be steep. Welders, plumbers, chefs, and others skilled in the trades can command good living wages. Those who provide the best service are typically those with considerable knowledge and skill and have the best interests of the customer at heart.

Sales and Marketing

The skills and concepts involved in business and entrepreneurship span nearly every subject area. Choose any topic and there is bound to be an industry built around it. Those interested in teaching could find themselves marketing education software. Many artists find themselves as commercial artists, owning art studios, or selling art. Even those interested in careers closely tied to charitable activities often work for nonprofit organizations, which also require a steady stream of income to keep operations going. Those working for nonprofit organizations therefore require similar sales and marketing skills as the local car dealers.

Customers and clients only invest in those that express confidence in their services. Selling is an act of persuasion, so business proposals lean heavily on speaking or writing skills, and often both. Those who prepare a business proposal that is poorly structured, or perform an awkward presentation, will raise concerns among clients who may choose to invest elsewhere.

Technical Consultants

Rather than the selling of products, many careers focus on technical consulting. Government agencies, for one, rely on technical consultants to inform officials on issues needed for the government to function. Offering professional advice on a complex issue involves considerable knowledge of issues related to the topic. Legal advisors, for example, understand existing laws and apply their experience to predict outcomes when new laws are drafted.

Planning consultants are paid to help others develop a plan for solving a complex problem. For example, a consultant hired to help a city beautify its downtown market can itemize what type of information must be acquired, what problems need to be addressed, who needs to be involved, and how to fund the project. In the end, such consultants draft a professional plan that guides clients toward achieving their desired goals. Such planning projects work well with classroom lessons because they focus not on being experts in a particular area, but rather knowing how to *acquire* the expertise and communicating that process to an audience. Such lessons serve to build metacognition, one of the KD components in our lesson planning scheme.

SAMPLE LESSONS

To model the lesson planning process, we will lean on six sample lessons spanning a wide range of subjects. These lessons are listed in table 1.1.

Sample Lesson A: Middle School ELA (Sports Journalism)

English language arts represents the most fundamentally important subject in K-12 instruction. For the sake of providing an example aligned to the Common Core, let us highlight a standard that addresses a topic favored among English teachers, namely *metaphors* (Common Core State Standards Initiative 2010).

Table 1.1 Sample Lessons Developed in This Book. Sample Lesson E Is Developed in the Chapter Titled Vignettes.

Sample Lesson	Grade	Subject	Subtopic	Standard
A	MS	ELA	Metaphor	CCSS-ELA
B	HS	Art	Sculpture/sketching	PASS (OK)
C	HS	Math	Statistics	CCSS-Math
D	MS	Science	Density	NGSS
E	HS	CTE	Civil Rights	CJS (NV)

> STANDARD CCSS.ELA-LITERACY.WHST.11-12.2.D—Use precise language, dimension-specific vocabulary and techniques such as metaphor [. . .] to manage the complexity of the topic; convey a knowledgeable stance in a style that responds to the discipline and context as well as to the expertise of likely readers.

We cannot hope to teach the entire standard in a single lesson. Rather, we will need to unpack the standard by focusing on a smaller subset of its objectives. Here, we will focus on "using metaphor to manage the complexity of the topic." We should notice that the verb in the standard is *use* implying that students should *create* metaphors to improve their writing. Simply asking students to *define* metaphors or *identify* metaphors in passages won't cut it.

> STANDARD CCSS.ELA-LITERACY.WHST.11-12.2.D (unpacked)—Use metaphor [. . .] to manage the complexity of the topic and convey a knowledgeable stance in a style that responds to the discipline and context as well as to the expertise of likely readers.

The unpacked standard includes the phrase "as well as to the expertise of likely readers," which means that words chosen for the metaphors must be understandable to those likely to read the written passages.

We need to also consider a career focus. Many students have a strong interest in sports, but many fail to see themselves engaged in sports as a career because they consider themselves unathletic. However, sports journalism is a viable career option, although the field is changing with the advent of social media and its shorter reporting cycles.

Metaphors are a mainstay of sports journalism (e.g., "The Four Horsemen"), so skill in their use often separates legendary sportswriters from ordinary hacks. Embedding a lesson on metaphors into the context of writing a sports editorial offers a great way to stimulate interest in English language arts among many students who fail to see a connection between core academic subjects and their own interests. In the lesson we will develop here, each student will be placed in a career as a sports journalist writing a biography of a famous athlete for the *Sporting News*.

Sample Lesson B: High School Art (Commercial Artist)

Teachers of noncore subjects such as music, art, and physical education also want to challenge their students but sometimes feel left out in the education reform discussion. So, for this example, we will choose an art education standard from one of the fifty states.

Which state? Having no particular preference for one state over another,[1] we will choose Oklahoma. In so doing, we will discover that the standards, in of themselves, do little to impact our ability to deliver rigorous instruction as long as we build rigor into the lesson during the planning process. Let us begin with a state standard rich in applications (Oklahoma State Department of Education 2006):

> HIGH SCHOOL ART STANDARD 3: Develop and apply skills and techniques using a variety of art media, and processes in making two- and three-dimensional works of art.

The verb *apply* in art education usually means having students create artistic works. Simply creating something doesn't necessarily align to the *create* category of the CPD. Here, however, the standards designers in Oklahoma cleverly used the action phrase "Develop and apply skills and techniques . . . ." To do so, students need to leverage academic knowledge in their creative processes, so the standard truly reaches the *create* category of the CPD. This standard goes on to list such media as drawing and sculpture as vehicles for students to display artistic expression. Why not incorporate both? Our unpacked standard becomes:

> HIGH SCHOOL ART STANDARD 3 (unpacked): Develop and apply skills and techniques using sketching and sculpting.

All too often the public envisions artists as eschewing all concerns for finances. This "starving artist" persona diminishes interest among students who, while wanting a career in artistic expression, also want to earn a comfortable living. Many artists want the freedom that comes with being an independent artist, but such a future requires some understanding of business principles.

One way to teach students business principles is through the act of writing competitive proposals. Although seemingly more suited for adults, even younger students can learn to write simple proposals to solve a real-world need. For this lesson, we will place students in the position as commercial sculptures wanting to compete for a lucrative contract. They will learn and apply some basic business principles in their proposal. Because business proposals are a form of persuasive writing, the link to English language arts is also strong.

Sample Lesson C: High School Math (Cost Analyst)

The CCSS categorizes mathematics along six major categories, one of which is probability and statistics. Consider the following standard (Common Core State Standards Initiative 2010):

> STANDARD 7: Analyze decisions and strategies using probability concepts (e.g., product testing, medical testing, pulling a hockey goalie at the end of a game).

The verb *analyze* points to the *analyze* category of the CPD. Of the three sample topics listed, we will concentrate on the first, product testing. Therefore, our unpacked standard is

> STANDARD 7 (unpacked): Analyze decisions and strategies using probability concepts related to product testing.

Students at both the K-12 and college level often fail to appreciate how strongly business depends on probability and statistics in its decision-making. We will place the student in the role of a cost analyst for a large-scale manufacturer. They will use statistics to estimate the total cost of a manufacturing process to see if their product is likely profitable.

Sample Lesson D: Middle School Science (Quality Control Engineer)

The NGSS incorporates a three-pronged approach toward building scientific knowledge in the classroom. Lesson plans should, whenever reasonable, address all three dimensions, which include (1) Disciplinary Core Ideas, (2) Science and Engineering Practices, and (3) Crosscutting Concepts (NGSS Lead States 2013).

One of the most common science concepts taught in both physics and chemistry is the concept of density. The NGSS treats density in a peculiar fashion. For fifth grade it states "density is not intended as an identifiable property. [Assessment Boundary: Assessment does not include density or distinguishing mass and weight.]" On the other hand, two sixth-grade NGSS standards (one for Earth's Systems and the other for Matter and Its Interactions) assume knowledge of density. So, a lesson centered on density, one of the most fundamental properties of matter, is standards-based.

One of the disciplinary core ideas for grade 6 addresses density (NGSS Lead States 2013):

> PS1-3. Each pure substance has characteristic physical properties (for any bulk quantity under given conditions) that can be used to identify it. (MS-PS1-3)

For this lesson, we will focus on the physical property, producing the following unpacked standard:

> PS1-3 (unpacked). Each pure substance can be identified through a physical property called density. (MS-PS1-3)

We will select some Science and Engineering Practices and Crosscutting Concepts for our lesson as we create its culminating activity in chapter 2.

Quality control focuses much of its attention on consistency of materials, such that one item leaving the assembly line is much like any other item leaving the assembly line. When items exhibit great consistency, this points to a high-quality manufacturing process. Reducing variability therefore is an important job for anyone focused on product quality. Quality control engineers are hired in industry to maximize product quality by focusing on measuring the physical properties of products. For some materials, a uniform density points to a high-quality production process.

For this lesson, we will place the student in the role of a quality control engineer, who will investigate the uniformity of a company's modeling clay by measuring the density of various samples to determine whether they vary significantly.

WHAT'S NEXT?

Now that we have selected a standard, topic, and career focus, we will next build a culminating activity to focus our students' efforts and demonstrate what they learned from the lesson.

NOTE

1. Don't believe that for a moment. Boomer Sooner!

Chapter 2

Culminating Activity

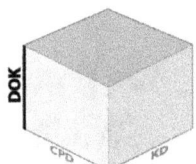

We now turn to the DOK axis of the Rigor Cube that drives Step 2 in the lesson planning flowchart in figure 2.1. Here, we will develop a culminating activity that will drive all subsequent lesson planning.

Not all lessons command the same emphasis. A math teacher may consider the teaching of factoring to be more important than polynomial long division. An English teacher may consider distinguishing between the active and passive voice a crucial skill but dismiss split infinitives as largely unimportant.

As discussed in the introduction, the four levels of DOK describe the degree of knowledge management required of students to complete a task (See table I.1.). Because DOK establishes the extent to which we expect students to demonstrate once they learn a topic, we can correlate higher DOK levels to increased topic emphasis. Therefore, lesson planning centers on DOK early in the process.

In a perfect world, all lessons would target high DOK levels. However, higher DOK activities require more time for students to complete, with DOK-4 activities sometimes requiring multiple classroom sessions. The school year is not long enough to teach all subjects to high DOK levels, prompting teachers to often make tough decisions about the emphasis for each topic. (A pacing calendar tied to DOK would form an ideal product for a teacher's professional learning committee.)

CREATING A CULMINATING ACTIVITY

The sample lesson plans developed in this book center on a culminating activity that guides students in their learning and provides them a vehicle for

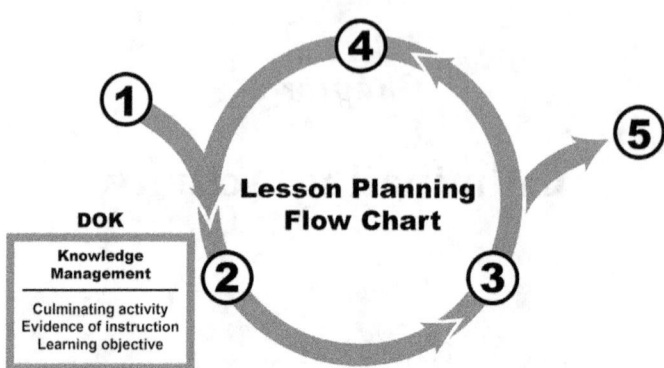

Figure 2.1   This Chapter Addresses Step 2 of the Lesson Planning Flow Chart, Where We Establish the Culminating Activity to Guide Student Participation. *Source*: Author.

demonstrating the knowledge they acquired. The scope of these culminating activities aligns to one of the four DOK levels.

How do culminating activities differ from the problem sets commonly found in a classroom? Consider a typical physics problem one would find in a textbook:

> A car of mass 1000 kilograms is traveling at 40 mph and needs to come to a stop within a distance of 200 feet. How much friction is required?

This problem involves only one beginning point (all of the values are specified for the student) and only one outcome (the calculated frictional force). Because so little decision-making is needed to carry out the exercise, such a problem aligns at best to DOK-2. Notice also the lack of relevance—why would students care how much friction is needed for the car to stop in 200 feet?

Compare this problem statement to a culminating activity of the sort we will develop in this book.

> A citizen is complaining that a certain stop sign does not provide adequate time for cars to stop and wants the speed limit lowered. City officials think the speed reduction is unnecessary. As a city civil engineer, you have been asked to investigate this claim. In a 10-minute PowerPoint presentation, detail precisely how you plan to settle the issue. Discuss all important factors that influence your analysis and how you plan to address each factor in your study. Provide sample calculations to clarify.

Such an activity places the student in the career ("As a city engineer . . .") and assigns a real-world task ("Develop a plan . . ."), therefore elevating relevance and engagement. The problem involves substantial decision-making (i.e., determining which properties will be important to measure, selecting the relevant equations). It also features multiple starting points (the physical properties needed to carry out the task are not stated for the student) and multiple possible outcomes (each student's presentation is likely to be distinct from the others).

Because of these levels of knowledge management, the DOK level most closely aligns to DOK-4.[1] Furthermore, students need to generate a product (the PowerPoint) and communicate their results to an audience (ordinary townsfolk who have little to no understanding of physics) other than the teacher.

Some will recognize the use of culminating activities akin to PBL. As described by the Buck Institute, PBL "is a teaching method in which students gain knowledge and skills by working for an extended period of time to investigate and respond to an authentic, engaging, and complex question, problem, or challenge" (Buck Institute for Education 2019). PBL is designed to stimulate creativity and critical thinking while students exercise communication and collaboration skills. Our lesson planning approach not only aligns tightly with the PBL process and goals, it goes even further, as we will see.

Creating culminating activities that target higher DOK levels does not always prove straightforward. Table 2.1 offers four basic approaches to generating culminating activities. For example, one way to teach students business principles is through the act of writing competitive proposals. Although this activity appears more suited for the older students, even elementary students can write simple proposals to meet a real-world need. As shown in table 2.1, one way to model the role of a proposal developer is to employ a simple algorithm: *You are working as a [job title] when asked for a [product/service]. Prepare a response, detailing why your product or service should be selected based on [concepts/skills].*

Using this algorithm, let us consider a culminating activity for a high school lesson on poetry.

> You are a freelance poet. The local police department wants to purchase a poem that officers will read at a fallen officer's funeral. Write a poem that you think meets their needs and a cover letter explaining the best characteristics of your poem (e.g., rhythm, rhyme, meter) that make it worth selecting over others.

The requirement to critique their own poem forces students to use what they learned in their previous lessons. To meet the above prompt, students would review what they learned in class regarding principles of design (e.g., contour, balance).

Table 2.1 Sample Roles, Culminating Activity Templates, and Examples.

Role	Template	Example
Analyst	You are working as a [job title] when you face [a challenge]. Prepare a solution.	You are working as a quality control engineer for a company that makes modeling clay. The density of the clay is supposed to be uniform (i.e., the same throughout the clay) but the owner is concerned that recent shipments have been erratic. Test the modeling clay and report to the owner your findings.
Proposal developer	You are working as a [job title] when asked for a [product/ service]. Prepare a response, detailing why your product or service should be selected based on [concepts/skills].	You are a freelance writer. The local police department wants to purchase a poem for the opening of a new headquarters. Write a poem that you think meets their needs and a cover letter explaining the best characteristics of your poem (e.g., rhythm, rhyme, meter) that would make it worth purchasing.
Dispute settler	You are working as a [job title] when a dispute over [issue] surfaces. Develop a presentation or report that examines both sides of the issue.	You are working as a policy advisor to a Congressman when a state proposes building two new nuclear reactor plants. The state wants the freedom to develop the plants but the federal government is objecting. Develop a presentation that examines the issue of states' rights from both sides of the debate.
Planning developer	You are working as a [job title] when [complex issue] surfaces. Develop a plan to study the issue. What are the issues? How can they be investigated? What would one look for?	You are working as a civil engineer when a citizen complains that a certain stop sign does not provide adequate time for cars to stop and wants the speed limit lowered. City officials think the speed reduction is unnecessary. Detail how you plan to settle the issue in a PowerPoint presentation. Discuss all important factors that influence your analysis and how you plan to address each factor in your study. Provide sample calculations to clarify.

Do artists ever have to worry about sales and marketing? Absolutely! The requirement that students develop a terms of agreement clause, an important component of business proposals, compels them to consider what happens when a client refuses to pay or is slow in paying. This activity would naturally blend into a discussion about the term "freelance," which would involve vocabulary development, salaries, the online freelance job market (e.g., guru.com), and the pluses/minuses of working as a freelancer.

Let us now consider the role of a dispute settler. As shown in table 2.1, an algorithm for selecting such a career focus is the following: *You are working as a [job title] when a dispute over [issue] surfaces. Develop a presentation or report that examines both sides of the issue.* Consider the following:

> You are working as a business manager for a company that promotes rock concerts. The marketing manager wants to borrow money to build a new web site for promoting events but the owner doesn't think the investment is worth it. In a business memo, settle the issue. Discuss all important factors that influence your analysis (including interest). Provide sample calculations to clarify.

Managers face such dilemmas all the time. The aforementioned culminating activity uses grade-appropriate mathematics (e.g., compound interest, simultaneous equations) to solve a real-world problem that students can envision doing someday. Students generate a tangible product (the memo) to communicate their results to others. (The above culminating activity does not provide actual numerical values for the principal, interest, and so on. Teachers can insert these values into the prompt if desired.)

Table 2.1 also lists the role of a planning developer. With planning activities, we do not expect students to generate solutions to problems, but rather to identify the most salient features of the problem. This allows students to tackle even the most complex problems without becoming buried by technological information. In essence, placing a student in the role of a planner, rather than a solver, shifts the focus of a lesson toward the more cognitively rich categories of the CPD.

For example, the effect on traffic of a new signal light is a complex affair requiring ample experience in traffic engineering. But students can brainstorm the issues that affect traffic flow without having to calculate the effect.

> You are a traffic engineer working for a city that wants to put in a new stoplight at a busy intersection that currently is a four-way stop sign. The city manager has asked you to conduct a study on whether the new stoplight will improve traffic flow. Develop a formal, written plan for conducting the study.

Part of the students' first tasks will be to ask pertinent questions such as the following:

- "What will we need to know?"
- "What will we need to measure?"

- "How would we tell if the traffic light improved conditions?"
- "How can we best explain our results to the community?"

Ideally, students would formulate these questions themselves. Otherwise, the instructor would need to provide them as guiding questions. Students would also need to discuss human response time, the timing of the stoplight according to the time of day and day of the week, fuel wastage, and so on.

Solving such a problem is difficult even for professional traffic engineers. A planning report, however, would only list those factors that would likely affect the solution. Students would still need to learn the fundamentals of traffic engineering. They would also need instruction on the scientific method, especially controlling variables.

Caution

Culminating activities cannot always be crafted for every lesson; the semester is simply too short. In many cases, topics should be covered in a single classroom session or even sooner. In such cases, the efficiency of direct instruction can develop the necessary skills and concepts in short order.

LEARNING OBJECTIVES

Many school districts require that teachers post learning objectives and recite them at the beginning of a lesson. A learning objective is an outcome statement that captures specifically what knowledge learners should be able to exhibit following the instruction. At minimum, learning objectives should specify an action verb and the main lesson topic. "Today, we will analyze similes" is one example, where the action verb is *analyze* and the main lesson topic is the *simile*. Some also feature a condition, which places the learning objective within additional context, usually placed in a prepositional phrase. For example, in the learning objective "We will describe trade in Medieval Europe" the prepositional phrase "in Medieval Europe" places additional conditions on the lesson.

Although lesson delivery considerations take place in chapter 5, we should note that the culminating activities we have developed form solid learning objectives in their own right. Reading the culminating activity aloud or writing it on the board will meet the basic requirements of a learning objective at most schools, but some discussion will help students address the task they face. For example, teachers should consider pointing out any new concepts or skills in the activity that may be new to the student and how the lesson will address this new content.

LANGUAGE OBJECTIVES

Language objectives specifically identify the type of language that students need to learn and use in order to accomplish the goals of the lesson. Language objectives ensure that all students can access the curriculum regardless of their English language proficiency (Himmel 2013). Although originally designed for English learners, their use supports all students because they insert purposeful language development into daily instruction and across the curriculum (Echevarria, Vogt, and Short 2008). Such language objectives, along with reading and listening, form the staples of most English language development programs such as Sheltered Instruction Observation Protocol (SIOP) and its public-domain cousin Specially Designed Academic Instruction in English (SDAIE).

For each activity, we need students to display their mastery of what they learned by providing a product that illustrates evidence of instruction. Most often, such artifacts of instruction appear in the form of speaking or writing activities, such as written reports or PowerPoint presentations. Naturally, we cannot expect students to exhibit skills in producing such artifacts without instruction, so we will be sure to include such support in our lessons.

In essence, by compelling students to produce artifacts of their instruction, we are incorporating important principles of English language development. New vocabulary words merit some mention as well. Even for native English speakers, English Learner strategies are especially effective for addressing unfamiliar words. For example, the contextual clue strategy of SDAIE allows teachers to briefly mention the definition of a word in more familiar terms as an aside comment.

Merely selecting the vehicle for student expression alone is insufficient to develop language skills. Later, we will devote our attention to the vocabulary and grammatical structures essential to carrying out the culminating activity.

SAMPLE LESSONS

With the above in mind, we now turn our attention to the sample lessons introduced in the previous chapter.

Sample Lesson A: Middle School ELA (Sports Journalism)

We now return to our ELA lesson on metaphors. Suppose a teacher considers the ability to create metaphors a key skill in writing, but cannot afford to spend the time needed to deliver a DOK-4 lesson. In such a case, DOK-3 may serve as a more reasonable alternative. In "Depth of Knowledge across Four

Content Areas," Norman Webb mentions one possible feature of a DOK-3 activity: "Students show awareness of their audience and purpose through focus, organization and the use of appropriate compositional elements." We can compel students to demonstrate awareness of their audience explicitly by incorporating this demand directly into the lesson prompt:

> You are a sports journalist for your own online blog. You feel that one of your favorite athletes has not received enough respect. You decide to write a biography of the athlete. Naturally, you want your biography to interest the reader, leave a lasting impression, and add to your portfolio for job advancement. You will choose two types of metaphors and use them to write a paragraph of a newspaper editorial describing how one of your favorite athletes impacted his or her sport. Then write a memo describing your metaphors to your audience.

Placing the writing of metaphors in the context of a sports biography helps reinforce the primary context of the standard, that is, "manage the complexity of the topic" and "convey a knowledgeable stance in a style that responds to the discipline and context as well as to the expertise of likely readers."

Requiring students to explain the impact of their metaphors on the reader (that is, the awareness of the reader) elevates the DOK of the question to DOK-3. To carry out this activity, students need to apply more knowledge about metaphors and take into account more information about the reader. (Simply having students create metaphors in a passage aligns closer to DOK-2.)

If required, a suitable learning objective associated with this culminating activity could be:

> Today, we will create metaphors.

We will emphasize the writing language domain, so much of the lesson will need to develop writing skills.

Sample Lesson B: High School Art (Commercial Artist)

Suppose an art teacher considers principles of design fundamentally critical to understanding sculpture. The teacher could then set DOK-4 as her student's cognitive goal. The Colorado Professional Learning Network (2012) provides a useful online resource for conjuring art lessons across all four DOK levels. For DOK-4, it offers the following:

> Students work as self-directed artists who use complex reasoning and planning. Students generate multiple correct answers to the artistic problems they set.

They choose and use art elements, principles, style, media, and techniques to achieve a desired effect.

Beyond just learning art as a skillful expression, students need to know that one can earn a solid living as a professional artist, but doing so requires some element of business savvy. It is not enough to make art; one must be able to sell it as well. Since we have chosen business principles as a worthwhile cross-disciplinary topic, then customer demands form an ideal way of expressing a "desired effect." Typically, customers place their demands to potential suppliers through email exchanges or phone calls. In the government, however, there are rules about procurement that often require a formal request for proposal (RFP). Because RFPs are common in business, this activity will provide an ideal vehicle for learning new vocabulary and how government agencies operate.

Considering all the above, we can formulate a DOK-4 culminating activity, spicing up the relevance of the activity by placing the student in the career field:

> You are a commercial artist. A police department has issued a Request for Proposals for a bronze sculpture dedicated to a fallen officer. Write a proposal containing a project design (sketch) emphasizing why your design should be chosen and the terms of agreement.

Contrast such an activity with something found in a more traditional lesson plan, such as having students sculpt with no emphasis on the principles of design and with no distinctive goal in mind. We instead want students to craft art that exhibits evidence of purposeful instruction.

For a learning objective, we could use the following:

> Today, we will sculpt to demonstrate at least four principles of design.

As with the earlier examples, the language objective is writing, which we can express as:

> Today, we will write a proposal.

Sample Lesson C: High School Math (Cost Analyst)

In this sample lesson, we will ask students to estimate the cost of shipping a large number of M&Ms if they measure the weight of a limited number of bags. Because the average bag weight of these bags only serves as an estimate of the true average M&M bag weight if they were able to measure the weight of every bag, students need to express the weight of the entire shipment in terms of confidence intervals.

> *You are a cost analyst for a candy company. The company plans to ship 10,000 bags of candy to a customer but needs to know the expected shipping costs. It costs 2 cents per ounce to ship. However, measuring the mass of all 10,000 bags is too costly, so the company provides 10 bags. You will prepare a cost estimate memo for the company and deliver an Excel spreadsheet to the manager. You will need to include the chances that the shipping costs could be higher or lower than you predict.*

To complete the task, students will use the cost-rate equation:

cost = cost/mass × mass/item × number of items.

Each student begins at the same point, with well-defined input information. Although each student team will use their own data, the output will be constrained by the rules of statistics. For this reason, this activity aligns closest to a DOK-2 activity.

We could express the learning objective as the following:

> Today, we will estimate the cost of shipping items using statistics.

As a language objective, we will concentrate on writing skills by asking students to write a memo, following the structure of a typical business memo. As a memo, this writing requirement reaches no further than the paragraph level.

> Today, we will write a professional memo.

Sample Lesson D: Middle School Science (Quality Control Engineer)

We have chosen to meet the NGSS standards by focusing our lesson on the concept of density.

> You are working as a quality control engineer for a company that makes modeling clay. The density of the clay is supposed to be uniform (i.e., the same throughout the clay) but the owner is concerned that recent shipments have been erratic. Test the modeling clay and report to the owner your findings, arguing for whether the manufacturing process needs improving or is satisfactory.

In this experiment, students will measure chunks of a large brick of modeling clay to see if the chunks have the same density. Naturally, the density of the chunks won't all come out to the same value. We can plot the values, however, and examine the overlap in data to determine how likely the densities are the same. In this lesson, students will use box-and-whisker plots and standard error bars for this purpose.

Note that framing the lesson objective in terms of a culminating activity meets four Science and Engineering Practices: (1) Planning and carrying out investigations, (2) analyzing and interpreting data, (3) using mathematics and computational thinking, and (4) engaging in argument from evidence (NGSS Lead States 2013). The nature of the topic at hand helps it meet certain cross-cutting concepts including Scale, Proportion, and Quantity (density is inherently a proportion) and Structure and Function (density is a fundamental property of matter) (NGSS Lead States 2013).

The learning objective could be simply,

Today, we will measure the density of a solid.

As a language objective, we will concentrate on speaking skills, which means that we will need to support students as they develop speaking skills.

Today, we will use effective voice inflections when speaking.

WHAT'S NEXT?

So far, we have completed Steps 1–2 in lesson development. We settled on a standard and topic, then crafted a culminating activity where students' will demonstrate their ability to meet the DOK desired of them. Next, we will address Step 3 of lesson development by identifying the content of the lesson plan students will need to learn to complete the culminating activities identified earlier. We will lean on another tool in our shop, the expanded KD of Bloom's Taxonomy.

NOTE

1. In practice, city engineers follow tables of codes and regulations when dealing with such issues as stop signs.

Chapter 3

Lesson Content

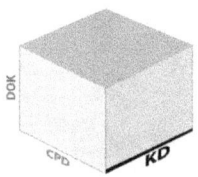

Naturally, *what* we plan to teach must enter the discussion at some point. We can generally classify lesson content into two major categories:

1. Grade-appropriate content—this is the content identified in state content standards appropriate for the grade level of the students. For any given lesson, such content can span multiple subject areas.
2. Background knowledge—these are the skills and concepts we expect students to possess before beginning the lesson (even though they often do not).

We will now address both types of content. Step 3 of the lesson planning process in figure 3.1 employs the expanded KD axis of the Rigor Cube.

GRADE-APPROPRIATE CONTENT

Lesson content has been traditionally split into concepts (which include facts) and skills. For example, a lesson on writing paragraphs would feature concepts (such as the structure of a paragraph) and skills (such as the procedure for completing a graphic organizer). Some subjects align more to concepts than skills, while others feature more skills than concepts.

The expanded KD of Bloom's Taxonomy we introduced in chapter 1 includes not only factual, conceptual, and procedural knowledge but also added a progressive touch by including metacognitive knowledge. Many educators in turn have supplemented the KD to reflect knowledge they consider critical to producing the "whole student" (Clark and Chopeta 2004, Clark and Mayer 2007). In chapter 1, we added to the original KD

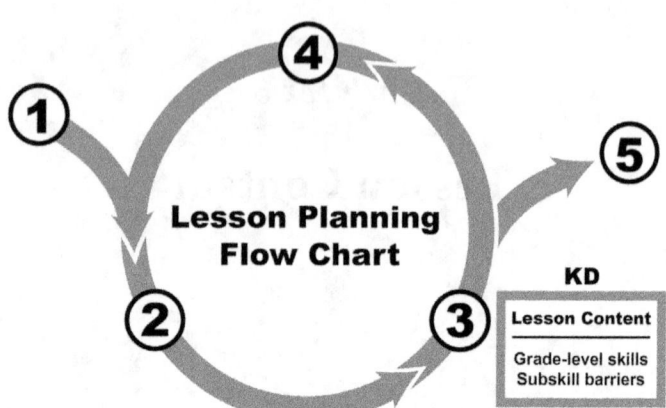

Figure 3.1 This Chapter Addresses Step 3 of the Lesson Planning Flow Chart, Where We Establish the Lesson Content. *Source*: Author.

as well by adding relevance knowledge and communicative knowledge to the list.

We will discuss once again each of the six components of our expanded KD but in more detail. Those interested in learning the following in more detail can consult with Anderson and Krathwohl (2001).

Knowledge Dimension Components

Factual Knowledge

What do we want our students to always *remember*? In other words, if our students were asked factual questions to test their knowledge on a subject, what facts would we want them to express correctly? Note that the depth of understanding exhibited by factual knowledge is lower than conceptual knowledge.

Anderson and Krathwohl listed two subcomponents of factual knowledge—knowledge of terminology and specific details/elements (Anderson et al. 2001). If we asked students for the definition of a quadrilateral, we would want them to state that it is (1) a two-dimensional figure, (2) has four sides, and (3) each side is straight.

We can liken factual information to listing the critical features of a concept. Critical features are those facts that combine to form the concept. The critical features of a chair include that it is used for sitting, has one or more legs, and has a back support. (Without the back support, the chair becomes a stool, a related but different concept.) The color of the chair, however, is not a critical feature as chairs can come in many colors. Therefore, factual development centered on the concept of chair would focus on its purpose and construction.

Conceptual Knowledge

What do we want our students to always *understand*? Conceptual knowledge corresponds to the interrelationships among the basic elements within a larger structure that enable them to function together (Anderson et al. 2001). This is unlike factual knowledge, which considers knowledge of facts in terms of isolated bits of knowledge. In some circles, conceptual knowledge is also called declarative knowledge, meaning that such knowledge refers to ideas that can be declared, that is, spoken or written.

Anderson and Krathwohl list three subcomponents of conceptual knowledge: (1) knowledge of classifications and categories, (2) knowledge of principles and generalizations; and (3) knowledge of theories, models, and structures.

People who have accumulated factual knowledge without conceptual knowledge know a lot of facts but only in isolation (i.e., factoids), but cannot connect them. (Cliff Clavin from the sitcom *Cheers* comes to mind.) Conceptual knowledge therefore involves expanding and connecting factual knowledge. Such subjects as history and government are largely conceptual in nature.

For example, conceptual knowledge related to the concept *quadrilateral* would involve not only knowing the definition of a quadrilateral but also that a rectangle is an example of a quadrilateral and so is a parallelogram. Conceptual knowledge would also involve knowing why an octagon is not a quadrilateral and which features an octagon and a quadrilateral share.

Procedural Knowledge

What do we want our students to always know *how* to do? Procedural knowledge refers to knowledge in how to proceed, not necessarily the skill in carrying out the tasks. It includes methods of inquiry and criteria for using skills, algorithms, techniques, and methods (Smarter Balanced Assessment Consortium 2015). Subjects such as mathematics and English language arts rely heavily on procedural knowledge.

Anderson and Krathwohl list three subcomponents of procedural knowledge: (1) knowledge of subject-specific skills and algorithms, (2) knowledge of subject-specific techniques and methods, and (3) knowledge of criteria for determining when to use appropriate procedures.

For example, procedural knowledge involved in analyzing the causes of the Civil War could involve students knowing how to select appropriate sources of information, how to filter the information according to whether they pertain to the causes of the Civil War, how to express this pertinent information in their own voice, and how to rank the causes from most important to least important.

A common mistake is to think that procedural knowledge always involves the *ability* to do something. However, as mentioned, procedural knowledge involves knowing *how* to do it. Procedural knowledge related to sculpture would not necessarily point to a person's artistic skill in sculpting, but instead the ability to shape their creations to satisfy principles of design. As such, students would express their procedural knowledge by explaining how they incorporated perspective into their design, even if their sculpture is aesthetically displeasing.

Procedural knowledge related to identifying whether a sentence is written in the passive or active voice would involve knowing the steps in identifying the voice (e.g., first, identify the subject of the sentence, then identify the action verb, determine whether the subject is performing the action, etc.).

Metacognitive Knowledge

What do we want our students to understand about what they *know* and *don't know*? As defined by Anderson and Krathwohl (2001), metacognitive knowledge involves knowledge of cognition in general, as well as awareness and knowledge of one's own cognition. Anderson and Krathwohl list three subcomponents of metacognition: (1) strategic knowledge, (2) knowledge about cognitive tasks, including appropriate contextual and conditional knowledge, and (3) self-knowledge.

For example, students studying physics can learn how to model the motion of an object hanging on a spring by examining the motion of a body rotating in a circle. They would also exhibit knowledge on why the mapping between the two physical models works and any limitations on the mapping. They would also assess their own knowledge of the motion by identifying what they think they understand and what they think they need to learn better, as well as how to go about learning this content. They would also identify how they would learn more about the behavior of springs to satisfy their own intellectual curiosity.

Relevance Knowledge

Why do our students need to learn the lesson? Relevance knowledge boosts engagement in a lesson by informing students of their "stake in the game." Students are more motivated to gain knowledge when they can relate to it. Relevance knowledge reassures students that they are in school for a reason. It allows students to synthesize multiple lessons into a bigger picture, slowly develop an appreciation for academic work, and link lesson content from lesson to lesson and grade to grade.

We can categorize relevance knowledge along four categories shown in table 3.1. In some cases, relevance can reach multiple categories. However, most lesson plans will focus on one or two.

Table 3.1 Taxonomy of Relevance for Teaching Students Why They Would Want to Learn the Lesson.

Level	Description	Examples
Personal/ Immediate	Students consider the lesson relevant to their current lives.	You will need to learn how to add decimals so that you can add money when you sell raffle tickets for new football equipment.
Personal/ Future	Students consider the lesson relevant to their future lives.	You will need to learn exponents because you will use it to compute the interest you earn on your bank account.
Professional/ Societal	Students consider the lesson relevant to society, even if they don't think they will directly benefit.	Scientists use the concept of photosynthesis to create alternative fuels.
Scholarly/ Academic	Students consider the lesson relevant to understanding the bigger picture of academic content, including satisfaction of intellectual curiosity.	We need to understand what took place in the Whiskey Rebellion to understand how our new nation was able to command respect from its populace.

Lesson relevance can reflect pragmatic or scholastic needs, but its application should extend beyond the students' coursework. For example, teaching students that many science fields require that authors write in the active voice while others demand the passive voice is an example of relevance development, as is teaching them that they can clarify their prose with the active voice and therefore help them get jobs. However, telling them that they need to learn how to write in the active voice to pass the upcoming exam, or that writing in the active voice is in the standards, is *not* relevance development.

Communicative Knowledge

How can our students inform others of their knowledge? Without communicative knowledge, knowledge is acquired for its own sake with little ability to impact society. Even worse, the lack of communicative knowledge stunts professional growth. We can define four general areas of communicative knowledge: (1) vocabulary, (2) speaking skills, (3) writing skills, and (4) presentation skills.

Unlike merely defining words (which is factual knowledge), vocabulary development involves planting new vocabulary into one's everyday working vocabulary. Therefore, students need to be comfortable writing words and pronouncing them, along with using words in context.

Lesson plans need to explicitly develop writing and speaking skills, and not simply mark papers for their adherence to writing conventions. For upper grades, this includes not only teaching students to write at the sentence and paragraph level, but also at the section level as well. (Each state specifies the grade level at which paragraph-level structure and section-level structure enters instruction.)

Speaking skills include myriad strategies including pacing, eye contact, stance/posture, intonation, and clarity. As with writing, such skills need development during a lesson, and not simply graded according to a rubric. So, during a lesson targeting speaking skills, a teacher could chunk her lesson by focusing on (say) eye contact, providing students with instruction prior to their speaking attempt and providing feedback on their ability to meet specified criteria.

Communicative knowledge also includes collaboration, such as teamwork and diplomacy, and presentation skills, such as effective use of charts and figures to convey information. As part of these presentation skills, communicative knowledge includes technical skills such as document formatting, the ability to display information in charts and tables, and the use of presentation technology.

BACKGROUND BARRIERS

Students may have not yet acquired some knowledge that lies outside the focus of the lesson, but impedes their progress nonetheless. Sometimes these barriers point to knowledge that we would normally expect students to acquire from everyday experience. For example, some students who come to class with little experience working with money could struggle in a lesson that involves cost rates.

Some background barriers refer to topics covered earlier in the year or in previous years. A lesson on creating paragraph transitions could disadvantage those still learning to write. A student performing a science experiment could struggle if they have not learned how to compute the average.

A good lesson must somehow scaffold these concepts and skills while allowing students to demonstrate mastery on the content specified in the KD. We will set aside such considerations for now and treat the problem with background barriers in chapter 5.

SAMPLE LESSONS

We are now at the moment to unleash the expanded KD on our lesson plans to nail down their content. Appendix B contains a template for developing the instructional content for any lesson. To demonstrate its use, we once again revert to our sample lessons. For reference in the later chapters, we will highlight those words that point to CPD action verbs (e.g., *remember, understand, apply*).

Sample Lesson A: Middle School ELA (Sports Journalism)

In our English language art lesson, we are designing our lesson around a DOK-3 culminating activity where students write a paragraph of a sports editorial describing one of their favorite athletes.

> You are a sports journalist for your own online blog. You feel that one of your favorite athletes has not received enough respect. You decide to write a biography of the athlete. Naturally, you want your biography to interest the reader, leave a lasting impression, and add to your portfolio for job advancement. You will choose two types of metaphors and use them to write a paragraph of a newspaper editorial describing how one of your favorite athletes impacted his or her sport. Then write a memo describing your metaphors.

To enhance the impact of their biographies, they are asked to employ two types of metaphors. To raise the DOK of the lesson, we are asking them to describe the impact of their metaphors on the reader. With this in mind, we could define the expanded KD as the following.

- Factual knowledge—we want students to *remember* that metaphors incorporate both a *tenor* and a *vehicle* and that a metaphor is an example of figurative language. (We could ask students to remember the definition of a metaphor as well. However, we will be asking students to *understand* the definition of a metaphor, which should suffice.)
- Conceptual knowledge—beyond just knowing the definition of a metaphor, we want to be sure students *understand* its definition and the definitions of *tenor* and *vehicle*. We also want students to *understand* that a metaphor is an example of figurative language, the definition of *figurative language*, and how figurative language differs from *literal language*. We would also expect students to *understand* each of the two types of metaphors they selected for their editorial.
- Procedural knowledge—the culminating activity makes it clear that an important component of this lesson is for students to *create* (or more specifically, know *how to proceed* in creating) at least two metaphors that responds to (1) the discipline and context and (2) the expertise of likely readers.
- Metacognitive knowledge—by the end of the lesson, we want students to *evaluate* their own proficiency, that is, what they have learned and what they have *not* learned. They should be able to *critique* their own metaphors with respect to purpose, creativity, and effectiveness. We would also want them to *draft* exploratory questions that will drive intellectual curiosity in their own leisure time.
- Relevance knowledge—we want students to *understand* that metaphors can make their current writing more interesting. We also want students to learn

that skill in creating metaphors will help them *understand* other writers' metaphors when they read them. We also want them to *understand* how this lesson can improve their chances of success in many fields that value creative expression (such as marketing).

- Communicative knowledge—students need proper vocabulary development on the most pertinent academic words in the lesson. They need to absorb the terms *metaphor, figurative language, tenor,* and *vehicle* into their working vocabulary, which involves being able to spell, pronounce, and use the words in context. The very nature of the lesson, creating metaphors to enhance literary imagery, promotes communicative knowledge in writing and, by extension, in speech. Because of the DOK-3 nature of the lesson, we can ask students to work in groups on the culminating activity, which also helps students learn communication skills. They should be able to critique the metaphors of their peers clearly but, above all, diplomatically.

We can catalog our expanded KD using the Lesson Content Table in table 3.2.

Sample Lesson B: High School Art (Commercial Artist)

We now turn our attention to the high school art lesson designed to teach students to respond to a request for proposals for a sculpture project.

Table 3.2 Lesson Content Table for Sample Lesson A.

Component	Students will . . .
Factual Knowledge	*remember* that a metaphor includes a tenor and vehicle
	remember that a metaphor is an example of figurative language
Conceptual Knowledge	*understand* the definitions of *metaphor, figurative language, tenor, vehicle*
	understand that a metaphor is an example of figurative language
	understand how figurative language differs from *literal language*
	understand at least two types of metaphor
Procedural Knowledge	*create* two types of metaphors that responds to (1) the discipline and context and (2) the expertise of likely readers
Metacognitive Knowledge	*evaluate* their own lesson proficiency
	critique the appropriateness/effectiveness of their own metaphors
	create exploratory questions for further investigation
Relevance Knowledge	*understand* that metaphors can make writing more interesting
	understand that skill in creating metaphors helps understand them
	understand that creating metaphors can improve career readiness
Communicative Knowledge	*use* the terms *metaphor, figurative language, tenor, vehicle* in daily life
	create metaphors to enhance writing and speaking
	work collaboratively in groups

You are a commercial artist. A police department has issued a Request for Proposals for a bronze sculpture dedicated to a fallen officer. Write a proposal containing a project design (sketch) emphasizing why your design should be chosen and the terms of agreement.

Upon completion of this DOK-4 culminating activity, we would like students to discuss the impact of business proposals on future careers, using art as just one example. We would also like them to evaluate other artists' work in terms of principles of design. Our expanded KD could look much like the following:

- Factual knowledge—what do we want our students to always *remember*? First, we need students to *remember* the names of at least five principles of design. (The Getty Museum 2011) Also, as part of their vocabulary development with respect to business principles, we want students to *remember* that RFP stands for Request for Proposals and that an RFP is a document that announces a need for services.
- Conceptual knowledge—beyond just knowing their definitions, we want students to *understand* the meaning of sculptor and a few select principles of design (e.g., *balance* and *contour*) as well as *describe* the impact of each principle of design on perception. Finally, we want students to *understand* what we mean by *terms of agreement*.
- Procedural knowledge—most pertinent to the art education standard, students should learn how to *apply* principles of design into their artwork. The culminating activity in this lesson also centers on *writing* the terms of agreement for a proposal, so students will need to learn this skill.
- Metacognitive knowledge—students will *critique* their own art in terms of principles of design, assessing its strengths and where it potentially falls short. We also want them to *understand* the limitations on what they learned about principles of design and terms of agreement and highlight some ideas on how they would attain this knowledge. To stimulate their intellectual curiosity, we also want them to *write* some exploratory questions that will prompt them to explore the topic further.
- Relevance knowledge—many students fail to appreciate the commercial side of art. We would want this lesson to change their perception such that they *understand* that art (in this case, sketching and sculpting) offers opportunities for viable careers. Along the same lines, we want students to *understand* why proposal writing, including the terms of agreement, is important to future careers.
- Communicative knowledge—as a DOK-4 problem, students will *collaborate* in formal groups over an extended time. We also want to fully develop their vocabulary development by learning to *pronounce* and *spell* terms related to the principles of design chosen for the lesson (e.g., *balance*, *contour*) as well as the word "sculpture" and its variants (e.g., *sculpt*, and *sculptor*).

Table 3.3   Lesson Content Table for Sample Lesson B.

Component	Students will . . .
Factual Knowledge	*remember* at least five principles of design
	remember that an RFP is a document that announces a need for services
	remember that RFP stands for Request for Proposal
Conceptual Knowledge	*understand* principles of design
	describe the impact of each principle of design on perception
	understand terms of agreement
Procedural Knowledge	*infuse* at least five principles of design into their sketch
	write terms of agreement
Metacognitive Knowledge	*evaluate* their own sketches
	write exploratory questions for further investigation
	understand the limitations on what they learned about principles of design and terms of agreement
Relevance Knowledge	*understand* how principles of design can improve art
	understand that artists need to market their creations
	understand the importance of terms of agreement
Communicative Knowledge	*work* collaboratively in groups
	use the terms *sculpture, sculpt, sculptor,* and whichever principles of design are selected in daily life

Table 3.3 summarizes the content for this lesson.

Sample Lesson C: High School Math (Cost Analyst)

In this DOK-2 lesson, students are estimating the annual shipping costs of a candy manufacturer, using bags of M&Ms as examples.

> You are a cost analyst for a candy company. The company plans to ship 10,000 bags of candy to a customer but needs to know the shipping costs. It costs 2 cents per ounce to ship. However, measuring the mass of all 10,000 bags is too costly, so the company provides 10 bags. You will prepare a cost estimate for the company and deliver an Excel spreadsheet to the manager. You will need to include the likelihood that the shipping costs could be higher or lower than you predict.

For this lesson, our KD could look like:

- Factual knowledge—this lesson centers heavily on inferential statistics, so we need students to *remember* the definition of a *sample* and *population*. We need students to *remember* the equations for the *mean, standard deviation,* and *standard error*. We also want students to *remember* that the population mean will (a) *most likely* reside within one standard error of the sample mean and (b) *almost certainly* reside within two standard errors of the sample mean.[1]

- Conceptual knowledge—it is not enough to know the equations for the *mean, standard deviation,* and *standard error*; students should also *understand* them. They also need to *distinguish* between a population (the total mass of the annual shipment) and sample (the total mass of an individual sample), as well as *understand* that the mean and standard deviations they compute from a sample are mere estimates of the population. We also want students to *understand* that the mean of a population will (a) most likely reside within one standard error of the mean of the sample and (b) almost certainly reside within two standard errors of the mean of the sample.
- Procedural knowledge—students need to *calculate* by hand the mean, standard deviation, and standard error for their data set of multiple mass measurements. Students will also learn to *use* Excel to *calculate* the mean, standard deviation, and standard error. They can then *predict* confidence intervals from the standard error to *express* their confidence in the total shipping costs. Finally, we want students to learn how to *format* their Excel spreadsheet for clarity, since the spreadsheet will be emailed to the manager.
- Metacognitive knowledge—students need to *monitor* their confidence as they undertake the lesson tasks.
- Relevance knowledge—the ability to forecast long-term expenses based on samples is highly valued in business. A thorough *understanding* of such statistics therefore can help students in a wide range of career fields, especially those related to large-scale manufacturing.
- Communicative knowledge—students must *collaborate* in pair-shares for this lesson. Vocabulary development will center on speaking and spelling *deviation* and *population*. English learners especially need to *remember* that the term "mean" is a homonym of two other meanings (*nasty* and the root of the word *meaning*).

What subconcepts or subskills could prevent our students from completing the culminating activity? Their math background could likely vary. The mass of each M&M in grams will undoubtedly be a decimal, but some students are poor in decimal arithmetic. Also, some students may not be familiar with finding the total cost when given the cost per item and the number of items.

Table 3.4 summarizes the content for this lesson.

Sample Lesson D: Middle School Science (Quality Control Engineer)

This DOK-3 lesson involves students determining the quality of modeling clay by examining portions of the clay for its consistency with respect to density.

Table 3.4 Lesson Content Table for Sample Lesson C.

Component	Students will . . .
Factual Knowledge	*remember* the definition of a *sample* and *population*
	remember the equations for the mean, standard deviation, and standard error
	remember that the population mean will (a) *most likely* reside within one standard error of the sample mean and (b) *almost certainly* reside within two standard errors of the sample mean
Conceptual Knowledge	*understand* conceptually the mean, standard deviation, standard error
	distinguish between population and sample
	understand that the mean and variation of a sample are estimates of the population
Procedural Knowledge	*calculate* the mean, standard deviation, and standard error for a data set
	use Excel to calculate the standard deviation and standard error
	establish confidence intervals
	format Excel spreadsheet professionally
Metacognitive Knowledge	*evaluate* their confidence in performing the tasks
Relevance Knowledge	*understand* how data sampling impacts business success
	understand that statistical analysis is used in a wide range of fields
Communicative Knowledge	*use* the terms *deviation* and *population*, in daily life
	remember that mean is a homonym of other meanings
	work in pairs

You are working as a quality control engineer for a company that makes modeling clay. The density of the clay is supposed to be uniform (i.e., the same throughout the clay) but the owner is concerned that recent shipments have been erratic. Test the modeling clay and report to the owner your findings, arguing for whether the manufacturing process needs improving or is satisfactory.

The central activity for this lesson involves students tearing chunks of modeling clay off a larger clay brick, then rolling the balls into spheres. By measuring the mass and volume of each sphere, they can determine its density.

This lesson assumes students have learned to find the volume of a sphere in a previous lesson from its circumference. To find the circumference of the sphere, they can simply wrap the sphere with a strip of paper and measure its length.

For this lesson, our KD could look like:

- Factual knowledge—the primary topic is *density*, so we want students to *remember* that the density of a substance is its mass per unit volume. This lesson centers heavily on statistics, so we could ask students to *remember*

the mathematical definition of the *average*.[2] To gauge the variation in data, we will use box-and-whisker plots, so students need to *remember* the structure of these plots (e.g., what the box represents, what the whiskers represent).
- Conceptual knowledge—it is not enough to *remember* the formula for density, students should also *understand* it. They need to *understand* that density is a proportion and is an example of proportional reasoning. Students also need to *understand* conceptually what we mean by the *average* and *variation*. Besides *remembering* the structure of box-and-whisker plots, they should also *understand* this structure (i.e., the boxes represent quartiles, which capture one-fourth of the data set, etc.). Finally, they should *understand* that high variation is represented by wide bars and corresponds to low/poor precision and that poor precision undermines confidence in measurements.
- Procedural knowledge—this lesson centers on density, so students need to know how to *solve* for all three variables in terms of the others. (E.g., given density and volume, find the mass.) Students need to *measure* the mass of each sphere. Measuring the volume is also an important skill, as students need to *measure* the circumference of each ball of clay, find its radius, and then find its volume. Naturally, not all portions of the clay will generate the same results for the density due to error and potential nonuniformity of the material. Therefore, students need to *calculate* the average of their measurements and *plot* the associated box-and-whisker plots by *analyzing* the spread of measurements.[3]
- Metacognitive knowledge—students need to *evaluate* their own confidence in understanding what a box-and-whisker plot illustrates, as well as what is meant by proportional reasoning.
- Relevance knowledge—students need to *understand* that quality control is a vital function of industry and is driven by statistical analysis. They need to *understand* that high variation means low confidence in measurements and therefore could lead to potentially high financial losses. A thorough *understanding* of such statistics therefore can help students in a wide range of career fields, especially those related to large-scale manufacturing.
- Communicative knowledge—as a DOK-3 activity, students can work in informal groups of (say) three. Vocabulary demands focus on using the terms "density," "average," "variation," and "whisker," "proportion," and "proportional" in daily life. The *spelling* of *whisker* needs special emphasis.

Table 3.5 summarizes the content for this lesson.

What background knowledge could prevent our students from completing the culminating activity? Students need to use the formula for density,

Table 3.5 Lesson Content Table for Sample Lesson D.

Component	Students will . . .
Factual Knowledge	*remember* that density is the mass per unit volume
	remember the formula for the average
	remember the structure of the box-and-whisker plot
Conceptual Knowledge	*understand* the physical meaning of density
	understand the average
	understand variation
	understand proportional reasoning
	understand the structure of the box-and-whisker plot
	understand the meaning of the statistical terms average and variation
	distinguish between the population and the sample
Procedural Knowledge	*measure* the physical properties mass and volume
	calculate the average
	plot box-and-whisker plots
Metacognitive Knowledge	*evaluate* self-confidence
Relevance Knowledge	*remember* that quality control is vital for industry and driven by statistics
	understand that high variation in measurements produces low confidence in measurement and that this low confidence could lead to large financial losses
Communicative Knowledge	*use* the terms *density, average, variation, whisker* in daily life
	use effective voice inflections

$D = m/V$, but could struggle solving for the unknowns m and V. Because it is background knowledge, their ability to solve for m and V in the equation does not constitute proficiency in this lesson. In chapter 6, we will see how to help them along in this regard without compromising the integrity of the lesson rigor.

WHAT'S NEXT?

We have now established the content of the lesson, which would meet the basic requirements of what many would consider a lesson plan. However, we also want to include the instructional strategies needed to deliver the lesson in the classroom. The choice of these strategies will vary from teacher to teacher. In the next chapter, we will present a wide range of instructional strategies from which a teacher can select, including a technique for overcoming background barriers.

NOTES

1. If so desired, students can use numerical values for "most likely" (68%) and "almost certainly" (95%).

2. The average is by far the most commonly used example of a mean. Although not exact synonyms, they can be used interchangeably at the middle school level. If the instructor chooses to use the mean instead of the average, students should be taught that the two words, for their purposes, measure the same thing.

3. Although students could use Excel to generate box-and-whisker plots, for this lesson it may be best for them to plot them by hand on graph paper to reinforce understanding.

Chapter 4

Lesson Delivery Methods

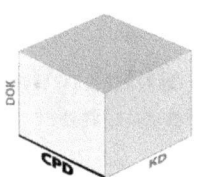

So far, we have established a culminating activity for our lesson using DOK, then established the content of the lesson using the expanded KD. But how can we teach this content? Oddly enough, the answer does not lie with DOK or the expanded KD but rather with the more familiar CPD, that is, the CPD axis of the Rigor Cube.

We now turn to Step 4 of the flow chart in figure 4.1. Because the content outlined with the expanded KD can span multiple subject areas, we will rarely rely on one instructional method for the entire lesson. Instead, we will use the CPD to align each content item in table I.4 in the Introduction to instructional methods we think will produce successful outcomes.

IMPACT OF THE CPD

Each lesson plan will likely encompass multiple categories of the CPD and possibly all six. The key to selecting instructional methods is to note that each instructional method works well with teaching some CPD categories, but not all. For example, a common middle school math lesson involves students discovering the Pythagorean Theorem through an instructional method called *guided inquiry*. For this lesson, guided inquiry could involve a series of graphical techniques that may span multiple classroom sessions. But if students are simply being asked to understand the Pythagorean Theorem and use it to calculate the sides of triangles, is this an efficient use of classroom time?

In short, lesson delivery requires continual dipping into the pedagogy toolbox. The more tools in the toolbox, the likelier chance that the teacher will have an effective, efficient method for teaching a specific CPD category. The result is a richer learning environment.

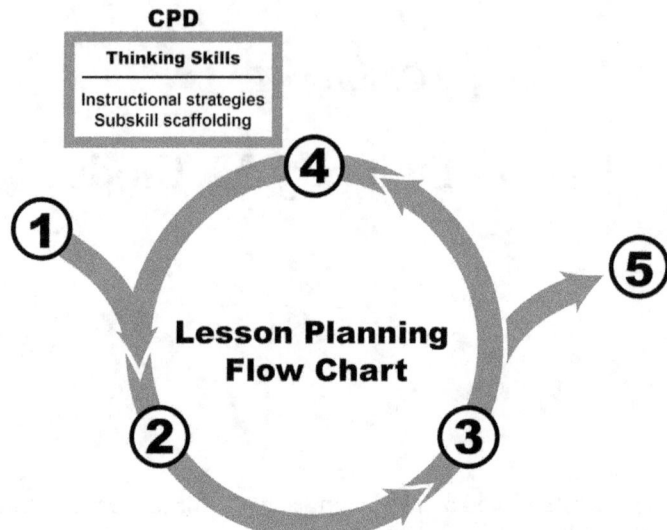

Figure 4.1 This Chapter Addresses Step 4 of the Lesson Planning Flow Chart, Where We Select Instructional Methods to Deliver the Lesson Content. Chapter 5 Addresses Subskill Scaffolding. *Source*: Author.

ALTERNATIVE BLOOM'S VERBS

In their revised Bloom's Taxonomy of 2001, Anderson and Krathwohl identified additional verbs associated with each of the six CPD categories (Anderson et al. 2001). These verbs are listed in table 4.1. As just one example, the CPD lists three verbs associated with cognitive processes aligned to the *analyze* category:

- *Differentiate*, which includes *discriminate, distinguish, focus*, and *select* (e.g., *distinguish between a law and a theory*).
- *Organize*, which includes *integrate, outline, parse*, and *structure* (e.g., *structure notes in preparation for writing an essay*).
- *Attribute*, which includes *deconstruct* (e.g., *deconstruct the writings of an author in terms of her political background*).

There is no shortage of resources for Bloom's verbs developed by educators (Teaching Innovation & Technological Support 2018, Lafreniere 2013, Shabatu 2018). Such verbs can prove useful in identifying the CPD category that is associated with a task, although we should note that the match is not always exact. We should also note that some of the Bloom's verb charts use the older Bloom's taxonomy of 1956. (If the CPD category

Table 4.1 Alternative Verbs Associated with Each of the CPD Categories (Anderson et al. 2001)

Category	Alternative Bloom's verbs
Remember	recognize (identify); recall (retrieve)
Understand	interpret (clarify, paraphrase, represent, translate); exemplify (illustrate, instantiate); classify (categorize, subsume); summarize (abstract, generalize); infer (conclude, extrapolate, interpolate, predict); compare (contrast, map, match); explain (construct, model)
Apply	execute (carry out); implement (use)
Analyze	differentiate (discriminate, distinguish, focus, select); organize (find coherence, integrate, outline, parse, structure); attribute (deconstruct)
Evaluate	check (coordinate, detect, monitor, test); critique (judge)
Create	generate (hypothesize); plan (design); produce (construct)

synthesis or *synthesize* appears in the table, the list of verbs is almost certainly obsolete.)

MAPPING INSTRUCTIONAL METHODS TO THE CPD

The chart below maps the efficiency and effectiveness of a few common instruction methods to each CPD category. For example, the rehearsal cognitive strategy is effective for teaching students to *remember* content, but a poor choice for teaching students to *analyze* content. However, guided inquiry is potentially a good choice for teaching content targeting the *understand*, *apply*, *analyze*, and *evaluate* categories.

The chart might produce howls among some educators. Some talented teachers can expand the range of a method beyond the CPD categories shown in the chart. This chart is a mere *guide* and will vary among teachers based on their experiences and skill sets. Like most guides, it is meant to be broken.

There are scores of instructional techniques that can help deliver content. In Appendix A, we discuss a few that we use in our sample lessons. Note that each of the instructional techniques alone can span an entire book, so all we can do is provide a superficial treatment. Much of professional development centers on acquiring skill in such techniques to expand one's teaching toolbox.

SAMPLE LESSONS

We can now demonstrate the use of CPD and figure 4.2 to select instructional methods using our previous sample lessons. We will collect these methods in tables using a template in appendix B.

Cognitive Process Dimension

Instructional Method	Remember	Understand	Apply	Analyze	Evaluate	Create
Cognitive Strategy (Rehearsal)	✓	✗	✗	✗	✗	✗
Cognitive Strategy (Elaboration)	✓	✓	✗	✗	✗	✗
Cognitive Strategy (Organizational)	✓	✓	✓	✓	✗	✗
Gradual Release of Responsibility	✗	✗	✓	✓	✓	✓
Think Alouds	✗	✓	✓	✓	✓	✓
Socratic Seminars	✗	✗	✗	✓	✓	?
Guided Inquiry	✗	✓	✓	✓	✓	?

✓ Potentially efficient and effective ? Efficiency and effectiveness uncertain
✗ Likely inefficient or ineffective

Figure 4.2 Mapping between CPD Categories and the Choice of Instructional Method.
Source: Author.

Sample Lesson A: Middle School ELA (Sports Journalism)

The first example we introduced in chapter 3 centered on a DOK-3 culminating activity where students spice up a newspaper editorial with figurative language:

> You are a sports journalist for your own online blog. You feel that one of your favorite athletes has not received enough respect. You decide to write a biography of the athlete. Naturally, you want your biography to interest the reader, leave a lasting impression, and add to your portfolio for job advancement. You will choose two types of metaphors and use them to write a paragraph of a newspaper editorial describing how one of your favorite athletes impacted his or her sport. Then write a memo describing your metaphors.

We already used the expanded KD in the previous chapter to itemize the lesson content for this activity. As students learn each item itemized in the table, they will employ certain types of thinking, whether they will be *remembering, understanding, applying, analyzing, evaluating,* or *creating*. We learned in the Introduction that the CPD categorizes each of these thinking types.

In the Instructional Methods Table in table 4.2, we have outlined the types of thinking (i.e., CPD categories) we expect our students to employ as they

Table 4.2 Instructional Delivery Table for Sample Lesson A

Category	Students will . . .*	Technique**
Remember	*remember* that a metaphor includes a tenor and vehicle	Rehearsal
	remember that a metaphor is an example of figurative language	Rehearsal
Understand	*understand* the definitions of *metaphor, figurative language, tenor, vehicle*	Elaboration
	understand that a metaphor is an example of figurative language	Elaboration
	distinguish figurative language from literal language	Elaboration
	understand the meanings of two types of metaphor	Elaboration
	understand how metaphors can make writing more interesting	Elaboration
	understand that skill in creating metaphors helps understand them	Video clip examples
	understand that skill in creating metaphors can improve career readiness	Video clip examples
Apply	*use* the terms "metaphor," "figurative," "tenor," "vehicle" *in daily life*	SDAIE
	work collaboratively in groups	Various
Analyze	None	None
Evaluate	*critique* the appropriateness/effectiveness of metaphors	Think-aloud
	evaluate their own lesson proficiency	Metacognitive Question Bank
Create	*create* two types of metaphor that respond to (1) the discipline and context and (2) the expertise of likely readers	GRR
	create exploratory questions for further investigation	Metacognitive Question Bank

* From the Lesson Content Table in chapter 4. ** Rehearsal = Rehearsal, elaboration, and organization stand for rehearsal cognitive strategy, elaboration cognitive strategy, and organization = organization cognitive strategy, respectively.

learn each content item in the table. Included in the table are the instructional methods that could be used to deliver the content. Let us now pore through this table row by row.

Remember Category

In this sample lesson on metaphors we want students to *remember* that a metaphor is one example of figurative language. An organizational cognitive strategy like the Venn diagram in figure 4.3 can help students remember this fact.

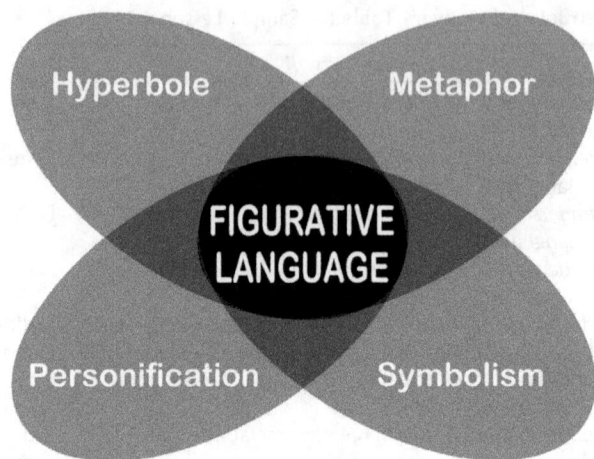

Figure 4.3 Venn Device for Helping Students Remember That a Metaphor Is One Example of Figurative Language. *Source*: Author.

How do we teach students to *remember* that a metaphor comprises a *tenor* and a *vehicle*? In this example, we can state that a metaphor contains a tenor and vehicle, then ask students to chant "tenor!" and "vehicle!" when prompted. To further entrench what they learned into long-term memory, we can ask students to write "metaphor = tenor + vehicle" in their notes. (Note the mnemonic "MTV," a rehearsal and organizational cognitive strategy.)

Understand Category

Sure, students may remember that a *metaphor* is an example of *figurative language*, but do they *understand* these terms? If not, remembering this fact alone will do them little good. And while we may not expect students to remember the names of every type of metaphor, it would be a good idea that they *understand* the definition of metaphor and at least two important types.

Figure 4.2 shows that we have access to numerous methods for teaching students to *understand*. We could use the direct instruction technique of instructional modeling, where we use examples and non-examples[1] to clarify the meaning of *metaphor* and *figurative language* and demonstrate to students how to *identify* at least two types of metaphor presented to them. We would also want to clarify what is meant by *tenor* and *vehicle*, again using examples and non-examples. Online video clips can also provide good examples of figurative language and metaphors, such as the example "Figurative Language in Country Songs (and more)" by Justin South (2014).

Short video clips where online content creators explicitly use metaphors to enliven their message can help students *understand* how creating metaphors can improve career readiness. One such example by the YouTube channel "How to Rap" discusses how metaphor is used in rap, which should resonate with many students in the class (Morisey 2014). Country music is another form of music steeped in the use of metaphor. (Buck Owen's song "Tiger by the Tail," which is easy to find on the web, features metaphors in almost every line.) Such examples not only reinforce relevance but they also expose students to new forms of music. Asking students to list songs on the web that feature metaphors not only reinforces the relevance of creating metaphors, it also provides a good check for understanding.

Apply Category

Beyond that, we would want our students to remember how to pronounce and spell *metaphor*, *tenor*, and *vehicle*, as well as their various forms, so they are more comfortable using the words outside of class.

The *apply* category extends beyond writing metaphors. We also want students to *apply* their vocabulary by using *metaphor*, *tenor*, and *vehicle* repeatedly throughout the lesson. Such a goal points to explicit vocabulary development, for which there are numerous techniques. Although not included in figure 4.2, Specially Designed Academic Instruction in English (SDAIE) provides a set of tools for developing vocabulary including contextual clues (for helping students understand the meaning of words), comprehension clues (for helping students know which words were spoken), and so on. Through repetition, use of these words will form a habit in their daily lives and they will begin to communicate more like professional writers and poets.

Analyze Category

While we could teach students to *analyze* the meaning of metaphors, such an activity is not expected of students in this lesson.

Evaluate Category

We want our students to evaluate the appropriateness/effectiveness of their own metaphors. Although the evaluation of metaphors is the stuff of serious research (Tourangeau and Rips, 1991), the evaluation of them at the high school level will be less sophisticated. As shown in figure 4.2, the think-aloud is often an effective vehicle for teaching students to evaluate (van Someren et al. 1994). Here, we can offer a sample metaphor "Winston Churchill was the bulldog of the pack," and verbalize out loud our thought processes as we evaluate the effectiveness of the metaphor:

Hmmm . . . one thing I want to accomplish is to spice up my writing using figurative language. The first metaphor I used was "Winston Churchill was the bulldog of the pack." I know that Winston Churchill is the tenor, because he is the man we are trying to describe with a metaphor. I chose a bulldog for the vehicle because, like Churchill, the bulldog is short and squat and has a grumpy, dour face. Also, the bulldog is a popular symbol of England, so that works, too. I also like the fact that I used the term "pack" to describe the meeting participants, which is also a metaphor. There is one thing I don't like—the bulldog may be short and mean, but is it a leader among dogs? Hmmm . . . I'm not so sure. Also, Churchill is compared to a bulldog a lot. Am I being really creative? Maybe this isn't the best metaphor to use after all. I'm going to have to rethink this one.

Following the think-aloud, we could ask students questions such as "What did I consider when I judged the quality of my metaphor?" and "What else could I have considered?"

Self-evaluation is also important. For example, students can ask themselves "What did I do to create my metaphor?" and "What can I do to write better metaphors?"

Create Category

The central activity in the lesson centers on students *creating* metaphors of their own. All too often, however, we expect students to simply start crafting their own metaphors once they learn the definition. But the *create* category requires concerted instruction in its own right. (Creativity is all too often considered innate and therefore unteachable.)

Teaching students to write metaphors is not simple. According to figure 4.2, GRR often works for teaching *create*-category thinking. In the first phase of GRR, we could model for our students how we write a metaphor to describe a celebrity of the students' choosing. (Until the final phase, the celebrity does not have to be a sports figure.) As a guide, we could incorporate a step-wise procedure by first writing a simile (which is typically easier) then recasting the simile as a metaphor by removing the word "like."

For the second phase, we would group students according to their ability (a form of differentiation) and assign them the task of writing a metaphor for a celebrity of our choosing, with the expectation that students, working in groups and heavily supported by our facilitation, will fashion reasonable metaphors. For the third phase, we can assign each student a celebrity, for which they will help one another develop reasonable metaphors. In the final phase, we can ask students to choose their own sports figure and create metaphors of their own.

In this lesson, the *create* category corresponds to students' producing metaphors that instill purposeful imagery in the reader. As students gradually learn to write metaphors on their own through GRR, they learn to evaluate the quality of their metaphors by listening to the teacher's think-aloud. Their own ability to create metaphors that enhance the appeal of their writing will also rise. Such elevation in real knowledge and skills is an essential building block of the *create*-category of the CPD. In short, the more you know the more creative you can be.

Finally, we want students to create exploratory questions they can use to drive intellectual curiosity outside the classroom. To achieve this aim, they can use the Metacognitive Question Bank in appendix A.

Sample Lesson B: High School Art (Commercial Artist)

Art instruction at the K-12 level often focuses more on craftsmanship and not enough on the cerebral aspect of art. In chapter 2, we devised a culminating activity for an art class centered on the principles of design (e.g., balance, emphasis, movement, pattern, repetition, proportion, rhythm, variety, and unity). Because artists need to sell their art, we embedded a business component into the following DOK-4 activity.

> You are a commercial artist. A police department has issued a Request for Proposals for a bronze sculpture dedicated to a fallen officer. Write a proposal containing a project design (sketch) emphasizing why your design should be chosen and the terms of agreement.

In chapter 3, we used the expanded KD to tabulate the content of this lesson in (as usual) the Lesson Content Table. Such a DOK-4 lesson will likely employ an extensive range of thinking skills on part of the students, which will, in turn, demand a wide range of instructional strategies on our part, as shown in table 4.3. As usual, we will now discuss each of the table rows.

Remember Category

Again, we can start by asking, "What do we want our students to always remember from this lesson?" Since the principles of design (The Getty Museum 2011) form the centerpiece of this lesson, we may want our students to remember them. To chunk the lesson, we can focus on only (say) four principles and reserve the other five principles for later lessons.

To reinforce recall of these principles, we can fall back on traditional rehearsal strategies, such as through choral responses or note-taking. The Internet also offers many mnemonic devices (Lynda.com 2019, Watercolor-painting.com 2019) for remembering the principles of design. Students could choose any one of the multitudes available, but why not let students create their own mnemonics?[2]

Table 4.3 Instructional Delivery Table for Sample Lesson B

Category	Students will . . .*	Technique**
GRADE-APPROPRIATE CONTENT		
Remember	*remember* principles of design	Rehearsal
	remember that RFP stands for Request for Proposals	Rehearsal
	remember that an RFP is a document that announces a need for services	Rehearsal
Understand	*understand* each principle of design	Elaboration
	describe the impact of each principle design on perception	Elaboration
	understand terms of agreement	Guided inquiry
	understand importance of terms of agreement	Elaboration
Apply	*write* Terms of Agreement for the proposal	Guided inquiry
	spell and *pronounce* each principle of design	SDAIE
	write exploratory questions	Metacognitive Question Bank
	use the terms "principles of design," "sculpt," "sculptor," and "sculpture" in daily life	SDAIE
Analyze	*analyze* impact of business principles on art careers	Guided inquiry
Evaluate	*critique* own ability to apply principles of design	Think-aloud
Create	*sketch* a sculpture that adheres to five principles of design	GRR

* From the Lesson Content Table in chapter 4. ** Rehearsal = Rehearsal, elaboration, and organization stand for rehearsal cognitive strategy, elaboration cognitive strategy, and organization = organization cognitive strategy, respectively. SDAIE = Specially Designed Academic Instruction in English

To teach students to remember that RFP stands for Request for Proposals and that an RFP is a document where an entity describes its need for services, we will employ straightforward rehearsal strategies by having students state these facts repeatedly either through vocal chants, answers to questions, note-taking, exit tickets, and so on.

Understand Category

We now consider the *understand* category. For example, we want students to not only know the principles of design, they should understand what each principle means. Teaching students to understand each of the chosen principles of design requires ample elaboration using examples and non-examples of artwork to clarify each principle. For this portion of the lesson, therefore, we choose the elaboration cognitive strategy. Fortunately, there are hundreds of web pages created by graphic designers and other artists for demonstrating each principle of design.

Few high school students have thought deeply about terms of agreement. But what happens if someone has failed to pay for over six months after the artwork has been finished and delivered, or rejects the completed product outright? Therefore, we need to introduce these real-world problems and teach these principles to protect artists when selling their artwork. Looking at figure 4.2, we see a number of techniques at our disposal. Here, the tried-and-true think-aloud is a good technique:

> I have to think, what can go wrong? Suppose I win the contract and go through the trouble to create the painting, but they reject the final product? Will I get paid? How much? That's a lot of work to go through for nothing. What if I ask for payment and it takes them six months to pay me? What can I do about this? What other issues are there that I'm not thinking about? How can I make sure I cover all bases? And could I scare off the client? I want to win the contract . . . maybe they won't choose my work if they think I'm being too inflexible with my demands.

Naturally, such a session should be followed by ample questioning such as "What were my concerns?" and "What issues did I consider?"

At this point, the teacher could ask students for their advice. Perhaps some students will suggest looking for websites that tackle this issue, or maybe find some sample agreements to examine.

Apply Category

How can we teach students to *apply* the principles of design into sculpture? Here, we can combine modeling with the think-aloud, sketching his or her own painting while using the think-aloud to illuminate his or her own thinking processes while completing the sketch. (However, we should probably shift the subject to something other than fallen officers, to avoid influencing students to emulate us rather than produce their own creations.)

> I want to somehow convey the idea in the viewer that the police department is always there for them. That it is stable . . . rock solid. I know that using symmetrical balance conveys stability, so I think I will begin with something that is symmetrical. I think having the police officer in the sculpture stand with both legs spread apart and his hands on his hips will convey this image of stability because of his symmetry.

As with all think-alouds, teachers should follow up with pointed questions such as "How did I incorporate balance into my sketch?"

How do we teach students to *apply* terms of agreement in their proposals? Here, we have selected guided inquiry as a good candidate, focusing in particular on the 5E model described in Appendix A.

- We can initiate *engagement* by questioning students on their present knowledge of terms of agreement. For example, are they aware of any examples where such terms are applied (e.g., software terms of use)? We can also allow students to discuss freely why they think artists need to learn business principles. We can ask them leading questions, such as "How promptly do you think you should be paid when completing a job?" We can even regale them with horror stories of what can happen to those ignorant of business principles (". . . and now Jimmy lives under a bridge").
- For the *exploration* phase, students can go online and perform Internet searches for examples, all the while determining which terms apply to their own projects.
- During the *explanation* phase, students can coalesce what they learned and prepare their first drafts of their terms of agreement while asking for input. Have they missed any important resources? Have they misunderstood any terms? Have they left anything out? Are they using all the key words at their disposal?
- During the *elaboration* phase, students consider the questions they asked themselves during the *explanation* phase to refine their terms of agreement, or search for ideas online to fill any identified weaknesses.
- During the *evaluation* phase students need to examine the impact of their terms for their own interests as well as the client's interests. Are they adequate to protect the artist? Are they likely to be familiar to the client? Will they cause the client to reject the proposal?

Analyze Category

Should artists care about sales? We want students to analyze the impact of business principles on art careers, which not only entrenches the relevance of the lesson but also will benefit students in their art careers. Here, personal exploration will likely work fine. Students can go online and see if famous artists have addressed this topic, or ask artists for their opinions. After this exploration is complete, they can even converse among themselves to brainstorm ideas that were not addressed.

Evaluate Category

We have emphasized the self-evaluation of one's own work as an important component of metacognition, and this lesson is no exception. Once finished, students should re-examine their artistic product in light of the principles of design. Rather than scoring the artwork for them, which would defeat the purpose of metacognition, we can help students self-assess their art through the think-aloud.

> Let me look at what my rough sketch . . . hmmm . . . I think my art features the sort of *balance* I intended. I wanted to convey a feeling that the police department provides stability and security, and I sketched the police building in the background. This building is symmetric and it is wide at the base. Sturdy . . . stable, those are the kind of feelings I get when I view my sketch. But, somehow I blew it when it came to *emphasis*. I wanted to emphasize the fallen officer's courage so I also sketched in the background a police badge, but it just doesn't come through. I need to work on this principle of design. Maybe I'll look up some resources on the Web.

Again, with the think-aloud we teach students to think *by example*. Also, hearing the teacher voice self-criticism helps those students too immersed in pride to admit mistakes, even to themselves. As always, we need to follow up the think-aloud with ample checking for understanding: "What did I look for when examining my artwork?" and "Where did I spot a weakness in my product?"

Create Category

By developing a deep understanding of the principles of design and learning to apply these principles to produce their own creations, students enhance their ability to create artistic products. They can boost their creative skills even further through student-centered exploration, examining online galleries and analyzing them with respect to the principles of design.

Sample Lesson C: High School Math (Cost Analyst)

As a DOK-2 lesson, Sample Lesson C involves fewer teaching strategies to deliver than other sample lessons.

> You are a cost analyst for a candy company. The company plans to ship 10,000 bags of candy to a customer but needs to know the shipping costs. It costs 2 cents per ounce to ship. However, measuring the mass of all 10,000 bags is too costly, so the company provides 10 bags. You will prepare a cost estimate for the company and deliver an Excel spreadsheet to the manager. You will need to include the chances that the shipping costs could be higher or lower than you predict.

The Lesson Contents Table for this lesson is shown in table 4.4.

Table 4.4 Instructional Delivery Table for Sample Lesson C

Category	Students will . . .*	Technique**
Remember	*remember* the equations for the mean, standard deviation, and standard error	Rehearsal
	remember that the mean of the population will most likely reside within ±SE of the sample mean	Rehearsal
	remember that the mean of the population will almost certainly reside within ±2SE of the sample mean	Rehearsal
Understand	*understand* the statistical terms "mean," "standard deviation," and "standard error"	Elaboration
	distinguish between the *population* and *sample*	Organization
	understand that the mean and standard deviation of a sample are only estimates of the population	Elaboration
	understand that the mean of the population will most likely reside within ±SE of the sample mean	Elaboration
	understand that the mean of the population will almost certainly reside within ±2SE of the sample mean	Elaboration
Apply	*calculate* the mean, standard deviation, and standard error	Elaboration
	use Excel to calculate the standard deviation and standard error	Elaboration
	predict confidence intervals for the population	I Do, We Do, You Do
	work in pairs	Pair-share
	format Excel spreadsheet for clarity	Elaboration
Analyze	None	None
Evaluate	*monitor* their confidence	Metacog Log
Create	None	None

* From the Lesson Content Table in chapter 4. ** Rehearsal = Rehearsal, elaboration, and organization stand for rehearsal cognitive strategy, elaboration cognitive strategy, and organization = organization cognitive strategy, respectively.

Remember Category

We can write the equations for the mean, standard deviation, and standard error on the board and have students write them in their notebooks as a rehearsal cognitive strategy. We can also write "most likely = ±SE" and "almost certainly = ±2SE" on the whiteboard and refer to them constantly.

Understand Category

To help students distinguish between a sample and population, we can employ a visual chart like the one in figure 4.4 and point/refer to it constantly throughout the lesson. ("Once again, the sample is a small portion of the population that we measure as an estimate.")

Ribbons like those in figure 4.5 can teach students to understand the mean by showing them how a strip of mean width produces the same overall ribbon

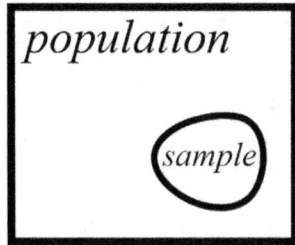

Figure 4.4 Organizational Chart for Remembering That the Sample Is a Portion of the Population. *Source*: Author.

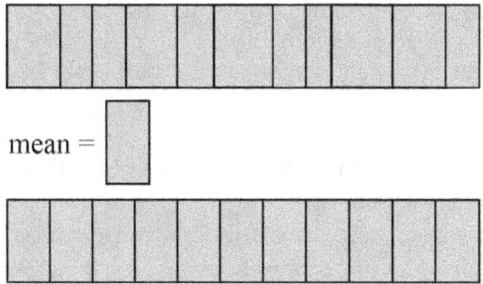

Figure 4.5 Two Ribbons Can Help Students Understand the Mean, with the Lower Ribbon Having the Same Length as the Upper Ribbon And Composed of the Same Number of Strips. When presented alongside grade-appropriate content. *Source*: Author.

width as the original strips of variable width. The standard deviation can also be represented graphically, where 68 percent of all measurements fall within one standard deviation of the mean. We can also explain that the sample error is a statistical tool that allows them to predict to a certain confidence the population mean from their measurements of the sample means. To reinforce this understanding, teachers can perform sample calculations on a given number of measurements and demonstrate how their results correspond to these definitions.

Apply Category

To teach students how to calculate the mean, standard deviation, and standard error, we can employ the I Do, We Do, You Do method while referring to the list of steps itemized on the classroom whiteboard. With this method, the teacher can lead off by performing the calculations on her own, then ask students to perform each step after she performs each step, and then ask students to perform the entire calculations on their own.

Students also need to use the standard error to predict the confidence intervals for the population mean. To this end, we can use the think-aloud;

First, I always get the standard deviation and standard error mixed up. I know my university professors did, too. I just gotta remember that the standard error is predictive; it tells me what the mean could be if I could take many more measurements. So, I have found the mean height of the students in my eighth-grade class as 65 inches and a standard error of 2 inches. But what about all the eighth graders here at this school? If I measured all of them and found their average, would I get 65 inches?

Hmmm . . . I think it would be close. But how close? Could I get 68 inches for the average? Maybe. 75 inches? Probably not. What about 55 inches? I don't think so. What would I likely get? What would I almost certainly get? Let me think . . . if I add and subtract the standard error from my mean, that equates to "likely." So, I'm going to do it! If I add and subtract 2 inches from 65 inches, I get a range of 63 to 67 inches . . . most likely. That means that the average height of all eighth-graders would most likely fall between 63 and 67 inches.

A similar portion of the think-aloud would cover adding and subtracting twice the standard error from the mean.

To format the spreadsheet for clarity, we can hand out sample spreadsheets and explain why they present data clearly, cleanly, and professionally. We can then show students using the I Do, We Do, You Do instructional method on how to format their spreadsheets using drop-down menus and keyboard commands. (Because we have chosen to teach students how to format their spreadsheets in this lesson, we cannot provide them templates for doing so.)

Evaluate Category

Students need to monitor their knowledge acquisition. Because this is a DOK-2 lesson, we should avoid absorbing too much time in this lesson. Therefore, the Metacog Log metacognition monitor in Appendix A will likely prove sufficient for this purpose.

Sample Lesson D: Middle School STEM (Quality Control Engineer)

We now turn our attention to the science lesson where students measure the density of a block of clay to determine its quality. The cumulative activity from chapter 3 is:

> You are working as a quality control engineer for a company that makes modeling clay. The density of the clay is supposed to be uniform (i.e., the same throughout the clay) but the owner is concerned that recent shipments have been erratic. Test the modeling clay and report to the owner your findings, arguing for whether the manufacturing process needs improving or is satisfactory.

Lesson Delivery Methods 55

The instructional methods associated with this lesson are tabulated in table 4.5.

Remember Category

The concept of density is central to this problem, so we can have students remember its definition. To reinforce recall of the definition of density, we can have students repeatedly write the formula and chant it in unison, both of which are examples of the rehearsal cognitive strategy.

Density is an example of proportional reasoning, which is the overlying concept. There is little for students to remember with respect to proportional reasoning (although they need to understand it). However, they do need to remember the steps used in calculating the mean. Once again, rehearsal cognitive strategy works well, such as writing a list of steps on the classroom whiteboard and having students recite the steps verbally.

Table 4.5   Instructional Delivery Table for Sample Lesson D

Category	Students will . . .*	Technique**
Remember	*remember* that density is the mass per unit volume	Rehearsal
	remember the structure of the box-and-whisker plot	Rehearsal
	remember that mean and average are synonyms	Rehearsal
	remember that quality control is vital for science/industry and driven by statistics	Rehearsal
Understand	*understand* the physical meaning of density	Elaboration
	understand the mean and variation	Elaboration
	understand proportional reasoning	Organizational
	understand the statistical terms mean and variation	Elaboration
	distinguish between the population and sample	Think aloud
	understand that the mean and variation of a sample are only estimates of the population	Elaboration
	understand that high variation in measurements produces low confidence in measurement and that this low confidence could lead to large financial losses	Elaboration
Apply	*measure* the physical properties mass and volume	Elaboration
	use the terms density, mean, variation, whisker in daily life	Organizational
	use effective voice inflections	Guided inquiry
	calculate the mean	Elaboration
	draw box-and-whisker plots	Elaboration
Analyze	None	
Evaluate	*evaluate* self-confidence in understanding the meaning of box-and-whisker plots	Think alouds
	evaluate self-confidence in understanding what is meant by proportional reasoning	Think alouds
Create	None	

* From the Lesson Content Table in chapter 4. ** Rehearsal = Rehearsal, elaboration, and organization stand for rehearsal cognitive strategy, elaboration cognitive strategy, and organization = organization cognitive strategy, respectively. GRR = Gradual Release of Responsibility

Understand Category

The conceptual knowledge tied to this lesson center on the concepts of proportional reasoning. In this lesson, if the density of the material is constant, then the ratio of the mass and volume remain fixed for any sample selected of the material. To teach conceptual understanding of proportional reasoning, figure I.2 indicates we can employ the elaboration cognitive strategy by providing examples unrelated to density but employing the same proportionality relationship. Part of elaboration strategy is to provide non-examples of proportionality, such as "On January 1, Bo was 10 years old and Jo was 14 years old. In ten years, Bo is 20 years old. That means Jo would be 28 years old. Right?" Students will guffaw at the logic employed, but having them explain why the reasoning is incorrect points directly to a misapplication of proportional reasoning, therefore, reinforcing understanding of the concept.

Apply Category

Finding the density of a substance involves applying the equation $D = m/V$. (Higher grade levels use the Greek letter ρ instead of D.) Students can therefore divide their chunk of clay up into smaller spheres, mass each sphere, and use $V = (4/3)\,\pi\,R^3$ to find its volume. Teachers can use the elaboration cognitive strategy, calculating example volumes on the classroom whiteboard.

From multiple measurements of the density, students need to calculate the mean and draw box-and-whisker plots to represent their data. Teachers can again use the elaboration cognitive strategy, performing multiple examples on the classroom whiteboard.

Students in this lesson will also learn to use effective voice inflections. There are numerous techniques for teaching students this skill, with the selection highly dependent on the teacher's personal preference.

Analyze Category

Students will also determine whether the size of the chunk they use to measure the density affects their results. They should have learned that it does not if they apply their knowledge of proportional reasoning. As part of this activity, therefore, students will uncover this fact on their own, a solid example of student-centered learning if they discuss their approach to confirming this fact experimentally among themselves. (If they are instead told by the teacher to break off various chunk sizes, that weakens the student-centeredness of the approach and potentially lowers its DOK.)

Evaluate Category

Should the density of each sample be exactly the same? If not, how much should the density of the material vary from one sample to another? Does this depend on how many samples are chosen? What would one do if the density of one sample is markedly different from the others? Tasking students with answering such questions serves as an example of student-centered instruction. A short Socratic method could come into play here, with the teacher directing students onto the meanings of the standard deviation and standard error as a way of incorporating the concept of variation into the discussion.

Create Category

This sample lesson does not involve the create category. If desired, students could be taught how to express their results in (say) a professional memo, but that could raise the DOK level of the activity and, therefore, take a longer time to complete.

PROFESSIONAL DEVELOPMENT

This chapter should instill the belief that professional teaching involves a wide range of instructional methods. Professional development can help teachers accumulate more of these tools and encompass both personal professional development and school-wide professional development.

For example, teachers not well-versed in Socratic seminars may choose to take part in workshops on this method, read literature, or consult with colleagues more experienced in its use.

Because such techniques as cognitive strategies and think-alouds appear in so many CPD categories, districts may want to establish proficiency in these methods district-wide to meet the district's broad initiatives.

WHAT'S NEXT?

At this point, we have employed a mixture of traditional and progressive teaching methods to deliver the lesson content. In the next chapter, we will remain on Step 4 but address the issues of background barriers, that is, content that does not constitute the expanded KD but could prevent students from demonstrating proficiency. Accommodating such barriers involves employing a form of instruction called *subskill scaffolding* that will allow us to teach grade-appropriate content while leaving no student behind.

NOTES

1. A simile is not a counterexample of a metaphor, as it is one type of metaphor.
2. This activity requires no external support or technology. As such, it serves as an ideal assignment for homework.

Chapter 5

Background Barriers

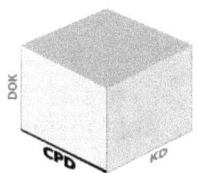

The previous chapter focused on Step 4 of the lesson planning process by establishing techniques for delivering grade-appropriate content. We remain on Step 4 in this chapter but shift our focus on those skills and concepts that students should have learned previously but perhaps did not. The central focus of this chapter is on an instructional technique called *subskill scaffolding*.

Students may have not yet acquired some knowledge that lies outside the focus of the current lesson, but impedes their progress nonetheless. Sometimes these barriers point to knowledge that we would normally expect students to naturally acquire from everyday experience. For example, if a teacher uses passages from Cinderella to teach a reading lesson, this could disadvantage students who have never read Cinderella nor seen the movie. Those students who come to class with little experience working with American money could struggle in a lesson that involves computing cost rates.

Sometimes these background barriers point to knowledge students should have learned earlier in the current year or in previous years. A lesson on creating paragraph transitions could disadvantage those who cannot write well at the sentence level. Students performing science experiments could fail to demonstrate what they have learned if they have not yet learned how to compute the mean.

> Such background barriers can undermine a lesson because many teachers think that students cannot learn grade-appropriate content without first learning the background knowledge. But they are mistaken.

As we detailed earlier, we want to adhere to a few fundamental rules and principles when identifying the content we expect to teach our students. Specifically, we want to

- define student proficiency purely in terms of the grade-appropriate content identified in the expanded KD and itemized in the Lesson Content Tables,
- carefully identify the background barriers that can prevent students from demonstrating proficiency on the lesson,
- avoid defining proficiency based on background knowledge not yet acquired,
- scaffold background knowledge for unprepared students, gradually increasing their proficiency on grade-appropriate content, and
- if at all possible, avoid subverting the Cognitive Rigor of our lesson plans.

NEED FOR SUBSKILL SCAFFOLDING

Traditional wisdom, fuels a mistaken notion that students cannot learn grade-appropriate content until they first learn the background knowledge related to the lesson. This appears to be a perfectly logical argument on its surface. After all, we have all heard the old saw "All knowledge is built on prior knowledge." When students cannot read, many naturally assume they cannot learn to identify metaphors in poetry. When students cannot multiply, some unquestioningly believe that they cannot calculate exponentials.

Severe consequences emerge. Rather than teaching students grade-appropriate content, teachers often reteach low-level subskills, in turn compounding the problem for students (and their teachers) as they advance in grade level. Besides capping learning opportunities, perpetual reteaching of low-level skills depresses student engagement and motivation. Students yearly endure reviews of basic skills, invoking the question, "If they haven't learned such skills by now, why would another round of exposure make a difference?" *It won't.*

PROFICIENCY DEFINED

Besides outlining the content of the lesson, the expanded KD also provides a good indicator of what constitutes proficiency on the lesson. For a given lesson, if a student can reasonably master each of the items in the KD, they have learned all that we can expect of them.

Consider a lesson on computing the exponential expression 4^3, which simply means $4 \times 4 \times 4$ (i.e., 4 multiplied by itself 3 times). For this lesson, the most likely subskill barrier is obvious: many students don't know how to multiply.

Sooner or later, however, we want students to provide the correct answer to 4^3 (i.e., 48). So, how do we teach students to compute such an exponential when they cannot multiply? The same dilemma arises in all subjects, especially when one considers how subskill problems with reading and writing can impact any classroom on campus. How can we teach students to identify the voice of a sentence (i.e., the active vs. passive voice) if they cannot even identify the subject of a sentence?

The key is to define proficiency only in terms of the grade-appropriate content that forms the focus for a lesson while setting aside concerns about proficiency on background knowledge. As we learned in Step 3 of the lesson planning process, this grade-appropriate content is established by the expanded KD.

Therefore, if students can state with understanding that 4^3 means $4 \times 4 \times 4$ and that this means 4 multiplied by itself 3 times, then they are proficient in the conceptual knowledge associated with the exponential. If they can express the procedure that to compute 4^3 you need to first multiply 4×4 and then take the result and multiply it again by 4, then they have expressed understanding of procedural knowledge *regardless of whether they can compute the answer correctly*. Multiplication does not form a component of the expanded KD for this lesson.

"Hogwash!" parents might complain. "How can you deem students proficient if they cannot compute 4^3 and get the right answer?" In response, could they compute 34^8 correctly? The chances are slim even for the most educated among them, but that does not mean they do not understand exponentials. They know what they are and know *how to go about* computing them. The fact that we might screw up the arithmetic when computing exponentials is therefore *completely irrelevant* to whether they are proficient in their computation.

The two computations 4^3 and 34^8 reside at the same Cognitive Rigor because they are both straightforward application of steps (i.e., DOK-1 and the *apply*-component of the CPD). By the same token, computing exponential powers of decimals (e.g., 12.4^3) is no more rigorous than 4^3 either. More difficult? Yes. More rigorous? No. So when students learn to compute exponentials, nothing is gained by using large numbers or decimals unless the standard calls for them.

Now let us consider a lesson on identifying the active and passive voices in sentences. A student who can state the definitions of the active and passive voices and can describe what is meant by these terms knows the facts and concepts. If he can also describe the process used to identify whether the sentence "The dog ate the homework" is active or passive, knows why doing so is important, and can communicate his knowledge to his peers, he has demonstrated proficiency in procedural, relevance, and communicative knowledge. This is all that is needed to demonstrate proficiency. A sentence like "The caterpillar consumed libations" could potentially mask proficiency for those students unfamiliar with the word "libations," a background barrier.

Reading skills form one of the most common background barriers. We should note, however, that raw reading skills only occasionally form part of the expanded KD of an English language arts lesson. In such case, reading sentences aloud to students while employing various reading comprehension strategies is an acceptable way to scaffold for subskills. Such an approach is especially effective for English Learners, who may not be able to read much English but still need to learn how to identify the active voice in a lesson.

SUBSKILL SCAFFOLDING

Naturally, we want students to perform 4^3 on their own eventually. Along the same lines, we want students to identify the voice of a sentence without needing help identifying the subject or action. State exams, which are often multiple choice and therefore unforgiving of background barriers, demand that students obtain correct answers. This is where *subskill scaffolding* enters the picture.

It is a common misconception to apply the term "scaffolding" to any instructional support. To be a true scaffold, there must be a process to remove the scaffold over time as students acquire proficiency. Therefore, the gradual removal of support structures over time is the essence of any scaffolding technique.

The term "subskill scaffolding" describes the process where teachers identify the subskills that pertain to a lesson and provide support structures to help students build these subskills in the short-term, while subtly teaching them these necessary subskills over the long term. As students acquire proficiency on the subskills, the support structures are removed.

The easiest way to explain subskill scaffolding is through examples. Consider the first step in computing 4^3, which requires students multiplying $4 \times 4 = 16$. Some students have not yet learned to multiply. Teachers can use rehearsal techniques such as whole-class chants to help students gradually learn basic multiplication facts for this first step. Or, the teacher can refer to a times table during instruction, allowing students to use their own times tables if they wish.

> Okay, with 4^3, we first need to multiply 4×4, then take the result and multiply it by 4. Let's do 4×4. We can see from the times tables that 4×4 is 16. Let's all repeat that. "Four times four equals sixteen." One more time, "Four times four equals sixteen."

Consider the impact on students' arithmetic skills from a full year of the teacher having them chant basic multiplication facts. Will many of them slowly acquire the multiplication skills on their own? Probably. (Notice that allowing students to use calculators does allow students to sidestep the background barrier, but doing so is not an example of scaffolding because the use of calculators does not help students acquire multiplication skills over time.)

For the last step (i.e., $16 \times 4 = 48$), the teacher can perform the multiplication on the board, voicing the steps out loud.

> Okay, so let me do this one for you on the board. We line up 16 and the 4 underneath the 6. Next, we multiply 6×4 and, using the times tables, get 24. We place the 4 under the 4 and place the 2 above the 1.[1]

Once finished, the teacher can check for understanding of their ability to perform these steps to gauge proficiency in the student's background knowledge. However, student answers to the teacher's questions should not count toward proficiency, which is defined only according to the grade-appropriate content in the expanded KD.

Over time, students gradually learn to perform the multiplication on their own. As they do, the teacher can shift away from performing the multiplication for them and ask them to perform more and more of the procedural steps. For example, the teacher can remove multiplication tables once students learn to compute the first step in the exponential computation. Later, the teacher can ask students to compute the second step on their own as well. If students stumble, the scaffolding goes back up and so the teacher reverts to computing the second step on the board.

Consider again the example of a lesson on identifying whether a sentence is cast in the active or passive voice. Here, a teacher could identify the subject of a sentence using the elaboration cognitive strategy:

> Class, how about an example? Consider "The dog ate my homework." Now, I'm going to circle "the dog," for you, because that's what the sentence is about. The sentence tells the reader what my dog did. So "the dog" is the subject of the sentence. What did the dog do? It ate. So "ate" is the action verb. I'm going to underline "ate." Now, I want each of you to take a few seconds and write down whether this sentence is active or passive. Also, write down the steps I took to identify whether the sentence is active or passive. Compare your results with your partner.

For this lesson, however, proficiency rests on whether students know (1) what the *active voice* and *passive voice* mean and (2) how to proceed in identifying whether a sentence is active or passive (i.e., what are the steps?). Over time, students will learn to identify the subject and action of the sentence on their own if they see enough examples like the one above. Once they do, the teacher no longer needs to employ the subskill scaffold.

Therefore, identifying those subskill barriers that could prevent students from learning grade-appropriate content forms a critical component of lesson planning. Teachers need to consider various means of scaffolding those subskills to keep grade-appropriate instruction on track and allow all students to access challenging, rigorous learning content. In short, subskill scaffolding teaches students grade-appropriate content while teaching students to build background knowledge *on the sly*.

For those still unsure as to how subskill scaffolding works, consider this example from English Language Arts on tracing the evolution of the bases and roots through time:

- Instructional Coach: "Your lesson was not grade-level. An eighth-grade lesson would have students trace the evolution of the bases and roots through time and note the way in which history influences their meaning, not to simply identify bases and roots."
- Teacher: "I know, but my students can't identify the base and root words in a word. So how can they even begin to trace their evolution?"
- Instructional Coach: "Well, why not identify the bases and roots for them? Can you circle the base or root and then show them how to trace its evolution through time using a dictionary? Comparing its evolution to important events in history would teach them that the content they learn in English is very much tied to what they learn in history. And, they would learn that words constantly evolve in time. Maybe for homework you could also have them predict what the word would look like in the future, which should be fun."
- Teacher: "Is circling the base word or root word acceptable? Can I do that?"
- Instructional Coach: "Sure! What does the standard want them to learn? How to *trace* the evolution of the bases and roots through time, not how to *identify* the roots and bases. That was last year."
- Teacher: "But I can't do that for them when they're taking the state test!"
- Instructional Coach: "Okay, while circling the bases or roots, could you describe why the words you are circling are roots or bases? And if you did that enough, wouldn't they learn to do that eventually on their own?"

The last statement by the Instructional Coach is the essence of subskill scaffolding. Students are learning grade-appropriate content while learning subconcepts and subskills as they go along.

PROFICIENCY ON STATE TESTS

Naturally, the issue of state test score proficiency rises up. Most teachers feel some pressure to exhibit high proficiency on state tests. Some feel *a lot* of pressure.

Subskill scaffolding accommodates a student's weakness in subskills and subconcepts by shifting proficiency on the lesson squarely on grade-appropriate content. However, a state test item could involve these subskills and subconcepts, even if the goal of the item is not to test them. For example, a state test could ask students to compute $(1.2)^3$. However, suppose we have focused the lesson on (a) knowing what an exponential means and (b) knowing the process in computing the exponential. Throughout the semester, we have scaffolded for decimal multiplication by performing it on the side, hoping that our students would pick up the skill through osmosis. But some students may still flounder on decimal multiplication. Have we failed them?

The answer is no. Thanks to our lesson, they know what the exponential is and they know how to go about computing it. Perhaps some students will round the decimals to whole numbers and figure the correct answer will be close to their result. Others might use an educated guess and put some bounds on the range for an acceptable answer. Still others will struggle but somehow get it right. Through subskill scaffolding we are giving them at least *a chance* on getting the correct answer.

Now, consider the case where we decided not to teach exponentials but instead focus on low-level multiplication. When faced with $(1.2)^3$, students have no chance at all. Even if they managed to somehow pick up the skill of decimal arithmetic, they have no chance of answering the question correctly because they have not been taught what an expression like $(1.2)^3$ means.

By the same token, a student who has had his history teacher read passages aloud when taught the fundamentals of the Gettysburg Address has a chance of scoring proficiently on this portion of the state test if the teacher has scaffolded reading skills throughout the semester. So, should history teachers scaffold reading skills throughout the semester? Absolutely! (By the same token, should science teachers scaffold writing skills throughout the semester? Absolutely!)

Addressing the problem of background barriers forms a critical component of lesson planning. We need to scaffold those subskills to keep instruction on track and allow all students to access challenging, rigorous learning content. When spiraling older content in subsequent lessons, teachers can elevate the difficulty of the tasks toward that anticipated on state exams. For example, when revisiting the lesson on identifying the active voice in sentences, subsequent lessons could focus on more complex sentence structures, such as compound sentences and sentences with implied subjects.

SAMPLE LESSONS

We now return to the sample lessons and discuss how to apply subskill scaffolding for each one.

Sample Lesson A: Middle School ELA (Sports Journalism)

This lesson centers on learning to apply metaphors to enhance a biography about a sports celebrity. The culminating activity is:

> You are a sports journalist for your own online blog. You feel that one of your favorite athletes has not received enough respect. You decide to write a biography of the athlete. Naturally, you want your biography to interest the reader, leave a lasting impression, and add to your portfolio for job advancement. You will choose two types of metaphors and use them to write a paragraph of a newspaper editorial describing how one of your favorite athletes impacted his or her sport. Then write a memo describing your metaphors.

Proficiency Defined

The dominant focus of procedural knowledge is on students knowing the process of creating metaphors to meet a literary need, even if the metaphors they create are of low quality. For conceptual knowledge, we want students to be able to explain the meaning of their metaphors and why they think they are effective. Beyond that, we want students to know why creating metaphors is worth learning, as well as how to collaborate with their peers.

Subskill Scaffolding

Are there any background barriers that could prove troublesome for students as they complete the lesson? Any lesson centered on writing immediately raises the possibility of a background barrier with respect to writing skills. Simply put, many students have not yet learned to write well, whether this deficiency results from substandard instruction in earlier grade levels, learning disabilities, or unfamiliarity with the English language. Such barriers could mask proficiency in writing metaphors.

For those students who agonize over paragraph structure, teachers can help them fill out a graphic organizer for their paragraph and then, using the completed graphic organizer, structure the content of their editorial. (Many examples of paragraph graphic organizers can be found with a simple web search.) Because paragraph structure is not the focus of the lesson, teachers can support students to any desirable extent in completing the graphic organizer without compromising the integrity of the lesson.

Such issues as punctuation and spelling do not contribute to the expanded KD and therefore do not count toward student proficiency. Naturally, we want students to improve their prose by the end of the school year. How do we scaffold this lesson for prose while teaching grade-appropriate content? One method is heavily favored by the Writing across the Curriculum program. In this method, teachers draw a thick line under the (say) sixth line of the students' proposal and only mark punctuation and spelling to this mark, not below it.

Note that students are not marked down for spelling and punctuation for this lesson because neither are grade-appropriate skills. However, they can receive instruction on how to improve their punctuation and grammar on the side. Over time, the number of students included in the marking can be increased once students improve their prose. (See Sample Lesson B for an example of how the Writing across the Curriculum guideline is explained to the student.)

What about the memo portion of the culminating activity? This portion allows students to showcase their ability to evaluate the quality of their own metaphors. Students should use the terms tenor and vehicle appropriately and their responses should indicate that they know what a metaphor is. However, writing skills should play no role in their own grade.

Notice that we did not incorporate the structure of a memo in this lesson. If we had, then whether or not the student structured his memo appropriately could have played a role in his or her overall grade. For this sample lesson, however, we chose to set aside such considerations.

We can now provide a complete Instructional Methods table, as shown in table 5.1.

Sample Lesson B: High School Art (Commercial Artist)

In chapter 2, we devised a culminating activity for an art class centered on the principles of design (i.e., balance, emphasis, movement, pattern, repetition, proportion, rhythm, variety, and unity (The Getty Museum 2011)). Because artists need to sell their art, we embedded a business component into the activity.

> You are a commercial artist. A police department has issued a Request for Proposals for a bronze sculpture dedicated to a fallen officer. Write a proposal containing a project design (sketch) emphasizing why your design should be chosen and the terms of agreement.

Proficiency Defined

As stated earlier, art instruction at the K-12 level often focuses more on craftsmanship and not enough on the cerebral aspect of art. This lesson plan focuses

Table 5.1 Instructional Delivery Table for Sample Lesson A, Which Now Includes Strategies for Addressing Background Knowledge Barriers.

Category	Students will . . .*	Technique**
Remember	*remember* that a metaphor includes a tenor and vehicle	Rehearsal
	remember that a metaphor is an example of figurative language	Rehearsal
Understand	*understand* the definitions of *metaphor, figurative language, tenor, vehicle*	Elaboration
	understand that a metaphor is an example of figurative language	Elaboration
	distinguish figurative language from literal language	Elaboration
	understand the meanings of two types of metaphor	Elaboration
	understand how metaphors can make writing more interesting	Elaboration
	understand that skill in creating metaphors helps understand them	Video clip examples
	understand that skill in creating metaphors can improve career readiness	Video clip examples
Apply	*use* the terms "metaphor," "figurative," "tenor," "vehicle" in daily life	SDAIE
	work collaboratively in groups	Various
Analyze	None	None
Evaluate	*critique* the appropriateness/effectiveness of metaphors	Think-aloud
	evaluate their own lesson proficiency	Metacognitive Question Bank
Create	*create* two types of metaphor that respond to (1) the discipline and context and (2) the expertise of likely readers	GRR
	create exploratory questions for further investigation	Metacognitive Question Bank
BACKGROUND BARRIERS		
Apply	*write* sentences that meet writing conventions	WAC marking
	structure paragraphs properly	Graphic organizer

* From the Lesson Content Table in chapter 4. ** Rehearsal = Rehearsal, elaboration, and organization stand for rehearsal cognitive strategy, elaboration cognitive strategy, and organization = organization cognitive strategy, respectively.

on reasonable understanding of a few principles of design and the ability of students to apply these designs in sketches for a future sculpture. We also want students to understand the importance of these principles of design.

This lesson also features a writing requirement at the document level centered on business principles, more specifically the terms of agreement. We want students to understand what we mean by terms of agreement and why they are important.

The writing scope of this lesson encompasses document-level formatting—the manner in which the paragraphs are arranged with respect to each other, including the use of transition sentences to connect paragraphs together.

Subskill Scaffolding

Now we need to consider the students' background knowledge. For the writing requirement, the focus of this lesson is at the paragraph level. However, students may find writing at both the sentence and paragraph level troublesome, which therefore forms a background barrier.

Like Sample Lesson A, this activity does not focus on writing conventions or sentence structure. Scoring rubrics should therefore emphasize the content established by the expanded KD and de-emphasize the student's raw writing skills. The writing assignment focused on whether students developed reasonable terms of agreements and can describe what these terms are and their purpose.

How can we accommodate the subskill for writing? Again, the Writing across the Curriculum guidelines can play a role. We can draw the line underneath the sixth line and only mark corrections to that line. Once again, mistakes in writing conventions should not play a role in the student's overall grade. To accommodate the student's subskill for writing at the paragraph level, we can employ graphic organizers. Because neither sentence nor paragraph structure plays a role in the expanded KD, we can support the students as much as we want.

The result of subskill scaffolding in both sentence and paragraph level could look something like the following:

> Bo, as you can see from the top six lines, you used a comma splice in the second sentence. I would like you to go online and watch the video on comma splices. Afterwards, I'm going to ask you to explain to me what they are and how to avoid them. But you still got 90% on the writing portion of the lesson because your proposal is structured correctly. You would have received 100%, but you discussed the penalty for late fees before you even mentioned what they are.

We can reflect on how Bo would feel getting 90 percent on this writing assignment. In the past, he might have received one F after another because he couldn't form proper sentences. He is still getting instruction on how to improve his prose. But in the meantime, *he is learning grade-appropriate content*. Over time, the need for supports like the instructional video on comma splices can be removed, which is the essence of subskill scaffolding.

Some students are better at sketching and sculpting than others. The quality of the student's sketch does not form a component of the expanded KD and, therefore, should not factor into the student's overall grade. Rather, the student should be scored on the student's effort in meeting the principles of design. (One of the reasons we required only a rough sketch was to remove artistic craftsmanship with respect to sculpting as a mark of proficiency.) There is no need to accommodate the subskill with respect to sketching, although teachers could provide support for improving their student's artistic skills if they wish.

The complete Instructional Delivery Table is shown in table 5.2. Note that despite our best efforts, many students will consider demonstrating proficiency on this lesson difficult because of the abstract nature of the principles of design. Such an activity is worth repeating later in the year using a different subject.

Table 5.2 Instructional Delivery Table for Sample Lesson B, Which Now Includes Strategies for Addressing Background Knowledge Barriers.

Category	Students will . . .*	Technique**
Remember	*remember* principles of design	Rehearsal
	remember that RFP stands for Request for Proposals	Rehearsal
	remember that an RFP is a document that announces a need for services	Rehearsal
Understand	*understand* each principle of design	Elaboration
	describe the impact of each principle design on perception	Elaboration
	understand terms of agreement	Guided inquiry
	understand importance of terms of agreement	Elaboration
Apply	*write* Terms of Agreement for the proposal	Guided inquiry
	spell and *pronounce* each principle of design	SDAIE
	write exploratory questions	Metacognitive Question Bank
	use the terms "principles of design," "sculpt," "sculptor," and "sculpture" in daily life	SDAIE
Analyze	*analyze* impact of business principles on art careers	Guided inquiry
Evaluate	*critique* own ability to apply principles of design	Think-aloud
Create	*sketch* a sculpture that adheres to five principles of design	GRR
	BACKGROUND BARRIERS	
Apply	*write* sentences that meet writing conventions	WAC marking guideline
Apply	*structure* paragraphs properly	Graphic organizer

* From the Lesson Content Table in chapter 4. ** Rehearsal = Rehearsal, elaboration, and organization stand for rehearsal cognitive strategy, elaboration cognitive strategy, and organization = organization cognitive strategy, respectively. SDAIE = Specially designed Instruction in English.

Sample Lesson C: High School math (Cost Analyst)

This lesson addresses a high school math standard.

You are a cost analyst for a candy company. The company plans to ship 10,000 bags of candy to a customer but needs to know the shipping costs. It costs 2 cents per ounce to ship. However, measuring the mass of all 10,000 bags is too costly, so the company provides 10 bags. You will prepare a cost estimate for the company and deliver an Excel spreadsheet to the manager. You will need to include the chances that the shipping costs could be higher or lower than you predict.

Proficiency Defined

Despite being only a DOK-2 lesson, the expanded KD for this lesson is sizable. The KD for this lesson is mostly concerned with students understanding a few basic statistical properties and how to calculate them. They then use these statistical results as predictive tools for the population.

Part of this lesson focuses on developing skills in Excel, specifically on (1) using Excel to compute the mean, standard deviation, and standard error and (2) formatting Excel spreadsheets for a professional appearance.

Subskill Scaffolding

Some students may not understand how to compute the total cost rate from the cost per mass, average mass per bag, and the number of bags. Such a skill does not reside within the expanded KD for this lesson (although it could if so desired). To scaffold this subskill, teachers could write the equation "Total Cost = × Cost/Mass × Mass/Bag × Number of Bags" on the classroom whiteboard and then perform sample calculations to clarify. Over time, teachers could assign similar rate-type calculations to help students gradually build this skill. If students have received prior instruction in unit cancellation, this would be a good opportunity to show them how the units cancel in this equation.

Students may consider calculating decimals by hand a real trial. However, proficiency in computing statistical values rests on understanding the concept of the statistical value and how to go about computing it, not decimal arithmetic. Therefore, teachers can use simple numbers (such as 4, 3, 4, 4, 5, 3) for this portion of the lesson, allowing Excel to handle the decimals.

One portion of this lesson focuses on teaching students to format Excel for a professional appearance using I Do, We Do, You Do. However, some students may not have any prior experience with Excel and could find maneuvering through the menu options and cells difficult. One way to provide support for the inexperienced is to pair them with more experienced Excel users.

Naturally, we would need to monitor the pair-share discussions closely to ensure that the inexperienced users are learning Excel during the lesson. Otherwise, the more experienced Excel user would end up being used as a crutch.

One way to scaffold this subskill is for the more experienced student to model how he or she maneuvers through Excel; the more inexperienced user can then repeat the instructions to the teacher. Over the course of the semester, the inexperienced user should (hopefully) absorb this skill in using Excel.

Although many spreadsheets use color to spruce up appearances, this could be a disadvantage to color-blind students. Gray scale, however, evokes a professional appearance and will prevent students from getting carried away with tasteless color choices.

Table 5.3 contains the entire Instructional Methods for this lesson, including background barriers.

Sample Lesson D: Middle School Science (Quality Control Engineer)

Let us now consider the middle school lesson on density, which we have established centers on proportional reasoning:

> You are working as a quality control engineer for a company that makes modeling clay. The density of the clay is supposed to be uniform (i.e., the same throughout the clay) but the owner is concerned that recent shipments have been erratic. Test the modeling clay and report to the owner your findings, arguing for whether the manufacturing process needs improving or is satisfactory.

Proficiency Defined

This lesson focuses primarily on computing the mean and applying foundational rules of statistics to gauge the variation of density in a sample of clay. We expect students to understand that density is an example of proportional reasoning, meaning that the size of the chunk they measure should not factor into their density measurement. Finally, students should understand the importance of quality control and how variation in their density values corresponds to quality.

Finding the volume of a sphere does not factor into proficiency for this lesson although it could if so desired.

Subskill Scaffolding

The focus of the lesson is not on computing density—typically a middle school concept. Still, students may not know how to solve for unknown quantities using the definition of density $D = m/V$. In other words, given $D = m/V$, students need to be able to solve for the mass ($m = DV$) and volume $V = m/D$.

Table 5.3 Instructional Delivery Table for Sample Lesson C, Which Now Includes Strategies for Addressing Background Knowledge Barriers.

Category	Students will . . .*	Technique**
Remember	*remember* the equations for the mean, standard deviation, and standard error	Rehearsal
	remember that the mean of the population will most likely reside within ±SE of the sample mean	Rehearsal
	remember that the mean of the population will almost certainly reside within ±2SE of the sample mean,	Rehearsal
Understand	*understand* the statistical terms "mean," "standard deviation," and "standard error"	Elaboration
	distinguish between the *population* and *sample*	Organization
	understand that the mean and standard deviation of a sample are only estimates of the population	Elaboration
	understand that the mean of the population will most likely reside within ±SE of the sample mean	Elaboration
	understand that the mean of the population will almost certainly reside within ±2SE of the sample mean	Elaboration
Apply	*calculate* the mean, standard deviation, and standard error	Elaboration
	use Excel to calculate the standard deviation and standard error	Elaboration
	predict confidence intervals for the population	I Do, We Do, You Do
	work in pairs	Pair-share
	format Excel spreadsheet for clarity	Elaboration
Analyze	None	None
Evaluate	*monitor* their confidence	Metacognition Monitor
Create	None	None
BACKGROUND BARRIERS		
Apply	*Compute* cost totals	Rehearsal
Apply	*Multiply* decimals	Elaboration
Apply	*Maneuver* through Excel	Pair-share

* From the Lesson Content Table in chapter 4. ** Rehearsal = Rehearsal, elaboration, and organization stand for rehearsal cognitive strategy, elaboration cognitive strategy, and organization = organization cognitive strategy, respectively.

As a scaffold, students can use an organizational cognitive strategy like the one in figure 5.1, which can help students apply the formula—placing their thumb over the desired quantity illustrates its relationship (i.e., placing the thumb over the volume indicates that you can find its value by dividing its mass by density, $V = m/D$, etc.).

One weakness of the chart is that it only helps with equations of the form $a = b/c$, which represents only a small subset of equations. As a scaffold, we would want to wean students off the chart over time. Otherwise, the chart serves as a mere crutch.

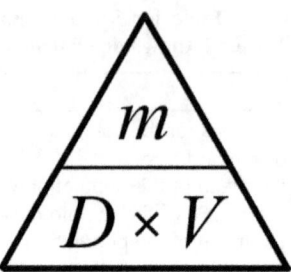

Figure 5.1 A Graphic Organizer for Helping Students Calculate the Density of a Substance. *Source*: Author.

The concept of mass should have been taught in middle school. As such, it represents background knowledge, not grade-appropriate content. We cannot expect all students to understand mass, so for this lesson we can define mass as "what a mass scale measures." Teachers can still discuss the meaning of mass throughout the lesson, continually voicing that the mass is a measure of a body's resistance to changes in motion. By the end of the lesson, students may be proficient in defining the mass. Regardless, their proficiency on this lesson should not rest on it.

The measurements that students receive will no doubt involve decimals. As a middle school lesson, the teacher could use this lesson as a vehicle for reviewing division by decimals or even teaching division by decimals. However, we have chosen not to focus on such division for this lesson so as to not overwhelm the student. Therefore, allowing students to use calculators is an appropriate aid for this lesson. However, we should note that a calculator is *not* a scaffold because its use does not help teach students to divide decimals. To scaffold this skill, teachers would need to instruct students on how to perform decimal arithmetic on the side. Again, their proficiency on performing decimal arithmetic should not factor into lesson proficiency.

Now that we have established both the grade-appropriate content and potential background barriers, we can discuss the lesson as a whole. See table 5.4.

FINE-TUNING

Once we complete Step 4, we return to Step 2 to fine-tune the culminating activity and instructional content, as shown in figure 5.2. This may entail adjusting the culminating activity, lesson content, or instructional method. Another adjustment we can make is to re-craft the culminating activity or the Instructional Content Tables to reflect the CPD verbs in table I.3. Although not necessary, the use of CPD verbs can make the lesson plan easier to evaluate by others.

Table 5.4 Instructional Delivery Table for Sample Lesson D, Which Now Includes Strategies for Addressing Background Knowledge Barriers.

Category	Students will . . .*	Technique**
Remember	*remember* that density is the mass per unit volume	Rehearsal
	remember the structure of the box-and-whisker plot	Rehearsal
	remember that mean and average are synonyms	Rehearsal
	remember that quality control is vital for industry and driven by statistics	Rehearsal
Understand	*understand* the physical meaning of density	Elaboration
	understand the mean and variation	Elaboration
	understand proportional reasoning	Organizational
	understand the statistical terms mean and variation	Elaboration
	distinguish between the population and sample	Think aloud
	understand that the mean and variation of a sample are only estimates of the population	Elaboration
	understand that high variation in measurements produces low confidence in measurement and that this low confidence could lead to large financial losses	Elaboration
Apply	*measure* the physical properties mass and volume	Elaboration
	use the terms density, mean, variation, whisker in daily life	Organizational
	use effective voice inflections	Guided inquiry
	calculate the mean	Elaboration
	draw box-and-whisker plots	Elaboration
Analyze	None	
Evaluate	*evaluate* self-confidence in understanding the meaning of box-and-whisker plots	Think-aloud
	evaluate self-confidence in understanding what is meant by proportional reasoning	Think-aloud
Create	None	
	BACKGROUND BARRIERS	
Apply	*manipulate* D = M/V equation	Organizational
Understand	*understand* mass	Rehearsal
Apply	*multiply* and divide decimals	Excel

* From the Lesson Content Table in chapter 4. ** Rehearsal = Rehearsal, elaboration, and organization stand for rehearsal cognitive strategy, elaboration cognitive strategy, and organization = organization cognitive strategy, respectively. GRR = Gradual Release of Responsibility.

REFLECTION

Now that we have established both the grade-appropriate content and potential background barriers for our lessons, we can discuss them as a whole.

The sequence of some of our lessons appear to follow the progression of categories in the CPD, that is, from *remember*, then *understand*, then *apply*, and so on. Such is not always the case. Teachers will need to decide for themselves the order in which they teach each component of their lesson. For example, it is often easier for students to understand a definition before

76   Chapter 5

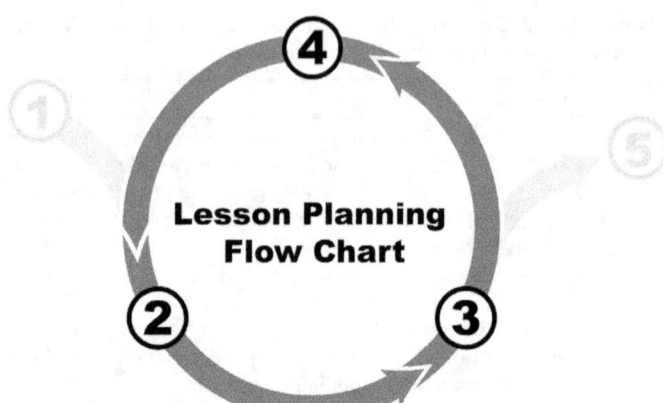

Figure 5.2 We Can Revisit Steps 2 and 3 and Recast Them in Terms of the Six Major CPD Verbs If So Desired. *Source*: Author.

they remember it. Some educators are now calling for students to engage in the *analyze, evaluate,* or *create* categories before the *remember, understand,* or *apply* categories. Because the CPD is not hierarchical, we do not need to follow any particular order when passing through its categories.

Note that these lessons involve a wide range of teaching techniques, both teacher-centered and student-centered, to complete their activities. Again, classroom instruction often features a melding of both types.

WHAT'S NEXT?

At this point, we have developed a lesson plan, which includes instructional methods for delivering it. We also took into account the need to build background knowledge and devised methods for meeting this need. But will students learn the content in our lesson plans? In the next chapter, we will focus on checking for understanding and questioning for engagement, two forms of questioning critical for successful deployment of lessons.

NOTE

1. This is the standard algorithm of multiplying large numbers. The best method for performing such multiplication is debated among math education circles. There is no need for us to join the debate.

Chapter 6

Formative Assessment

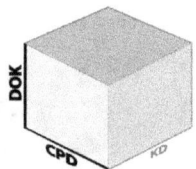

Assessment incorporates all that educators do to measure student learning. *Formative assessment* uses such measurements to provide ongoing feedback for instructors to improve their teaching and for students to improve their learning. In this final step of the lesson planning process, as shown in figure 6.1, we will focus on formative assessment by establishing questions that will help us check for understanding and boost engagement among students. We will also spend considerable space on techniques for delivering the questions to students. In short, we will use

- the CPD axis of the Rigor Cube to develop questions that compel students to practice a wide range of thinking skills,
- the DOK axis of the Rigor Cube to identify the wait-time and student grouping demands associated with questions and activities.

Formative assessment embodies a key component of instruction because it helps (Black and William 2001, Francis 2016, Eberly Center at Carnegie Mellon University 2019)

- students identify their strengths and weaknesses and target areas that need work and
- teachers recognize where students are struggling and address problems immediately.

Summative assessment, on the other hand, uses results to evaluate student learning at the end of an instructional unit. We will focus on formative assessment in this book because of its ability to impact instructional practice on a daily basis.

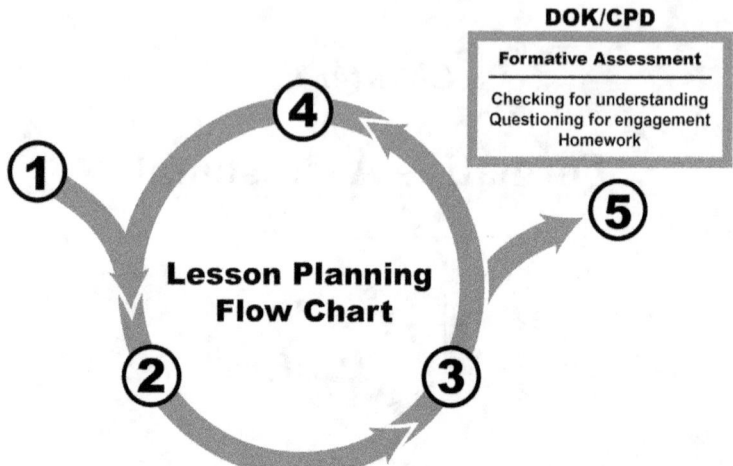

Figure 6.1   This Chapter Addresses Step 5 of the Lesson Planning Flow Chart, Where We Develop Formative Assessments for Our Lessons. *Source*: Author.

Research attests to the power of good questioning strategies for boosting student learning (Walsh and Sattes 2005, Albergaria-Almeida 2012, Walsh 2015). Classroom questioning also poses as perhaps the most correctable facet of instruction. We can transform classroom questioning into a strength by ensuring that assessment adheres to some fundamental guiding principles. Namely, classroom questioning should (Olvera and Walkup 2010)

1. engage all students,
2. continually measure student understanding throughout the lesson,
3. allow adequate time for students to conjure adequate responses, and
4. address how to react to students once they offer their responses to questions.

We question students during instruction primarily to perform two important tasks: Checking for understanding and questioning for engagement. We will now discuss each aspect of questioning separately. Then, we will introduce a systematic questioning strategy called GRAPPLE that will help align classroom questioning to the above four principles.

CHECKING FOR UNDERSTANDING

Teachers should often (and this means *often*) question students to check their understanding as they teach. Doing so allows teachers to gauge the effectiveness of their instruction and identify student struggle on a continual basis as the following analogy explains:

> Picture a vintage car that has a carburetor problem. If the driver steps on the gas pedal too quickly, the engine stumbles and quits. To get the car moving, the driver listens carefully to the engine. When the engine begins to stumble, she must back off the gas pedal. Once the engine begins to run smoothly again, she presses more on the gas pedal until it stumbles once again. By "nursing the gas pedal," that is, pressing on the gas pedal until the car stumbles, then backing off until the engine begins running smoothly, the car will eventually travel to the driver's desired destination.

Teaching is much the same. Students are like the vintage car with the bad carburetor. As long as the instruction is adequately paced, all is fine. Teach too much too fast (or ineffectively), however, and they stumble. Effective checking for understanding involves constantly monitoring proficiency by asking numerous questions and listening to student responses. If we hear students stumble, we need to back off by slowing down the instruction, often re-teaching content they failed to learn.

With checking for understanding, questioning often targets the *remember*, *understand*, and *apply* categories of the CPD. Checking for understanding searches for correct responses rather than opinion. For example, a math teacher could ask "what is the definition of the lowest common denominator?" to check for understanding of her student's understanding of factual knowledge.

Checking for understanding should probe hard to assess proficiency. One common method is to ask students to justify their answers. Students citing "he" as a definite pronoun may not understand the concept of *definiteness*. Is "he" in the famous quote "He who hesitates is lost" a definite pronoun? By asking students to explain their reasoning, teachers shine the light on student weaknesses and generate quality feedback on their own teaching effectiveness.

QUESTIONING FOR ENGAGEMENT

Some questions prompt students into engaging their academic content in meaningful ways. Such questions rarely seek correct answers, but rather sensible opinions. Although most checking for understanding questions target low levels of cognition, questioning for engagement usually involves higher-order thinking.

For example, a math instructor teaching a lesson on lowest common denominators could ask "Which is harder to find—the lowest common denominator or the greatest common factor and why?" Such a question has

Table 6.1 Contrasting Checking for Understanding and Questioning for Engagement.

	Checking for Understanding	Questioning for Engagement
Primary purpose	Gauge whether students are learning	Compel students to reengage academic content in new ways
Primary benefit	Paces lesson and ensures no students are left behind	Enhances critical thinking and student engagement
CPD category	Mostly *remember, understand, apply*	Mostly *analyze, evaluate,* and *create*
Response evaluation	Based on correctness	Based on reasoning
Student selection	Mostly random sampling	Mostly selection of volunteers
Student grouping	Usually individual students	Usually pair-shares or groups

no correct or incorrect answer. Rather, the *process* employed in arriving at a sensible answer serves as a learning activity in its own right. To answer such a question, students would need to peruse their notes or textbook, or discuss the two concepts with their classmates. This is just the sort of critical reflection we want to activate in our classrooms.

Table 6.1 summarizes the main differences between checking for understanding and questioning for engagement. We will discuss the rows corresponding to student selection and grouping a bit later.

DEVELOPING QUESTIONS

To assess proficiency at a deep level and stimulate critical thinking, we want to avoid asking only *remember*-category questions, a long-standing problem in instruction (Gall 1984, Francis 2016). Much research has found that higher-order questions correlate closely to higher student achievement (Redfield and Rousseau 1981) with low income and younger students benefiting the most (Gall 1984). However, we want to avoid getting carried away by neglecting low-order questions.

> To help students perform better on today's high-stakes tests, teachers should give students a range of opportunities to think—including knowledge questions as well as higher-order questions. (Walsh and Sattes, 2005)

Thankfully, many educators have posted numerous tips on creating questions that sample a wider range of Bloom's Taxonomy. Table 6.2 illustrates a few of these question stems—a simple web search using the key phrases "Bloom's Taxonomy" and "question stems" will generate plenty more (Lafreniere 2013, Francis 2016, Shabatu 2018, Teaching Innovation & Technological Support 2018).

As shown in table 6.2, asking a student "How would you summarize photosynthesis?" is a great way to enhance *understand*-category thinking. Asking

Table 6.2 Bloom's Taxonomy Question Stems.

CPD Category	Question Stem
Understand	In your own words, describe . . .
	How would you summarize . . . ?
	What is the main idea . . . ?
	How did we solve . . . ?
	Provide an example . . .
Apply	How would you use . . . ?
	How would you solve . . . ?
	Demonstrate to me . . .
	Apply ___ to your own experiences.
Analyze	How would you classify . . . ?
	What is the relationship between . . . ?
	What would be the impact of . . . ?
Evaluate	Which is the most important . . . ?
	Rank ___ in degrees of importance.
	What could be done to min/maximize . . . ?
Create	Create a scenario in which ___ applies.
	Write a short story that demonstrates . . .
	What choice would you have made . . . ?

the student "What is the relationship between sunlight and plant growth?" will promote *analyze*-category thinking.

We can develop *evaluate*-category thinking whenever we introduce a number of items pertaining to a lesson concept—simply ask students to select the most important item or have them rank the items in importance. (To raise engagement levels sky-high, consider asking students working in groups to form a consensus.)

> Students, we have listed on the whiteboard four rules for proofreading articles. In your groups, select what you think is the most important rule and why you made this choice.

Some of the questions in table 6.2 serve another purpose—buying time. Sometimes a teacher is not prepared to teach right away. Often, this can be a result of technology not working, or misplaced notes. Consider the following scenario, where a teacher cannot find her lecture notes and her students (and the administrator in the back of the room performing an evaluation) are waiting for her to begin instruction. Rather than apologizing, the teacher can dial up one of the questions from table 6.2.

> Students, I want you to go through your notes, talk about what we learned with your peer buddy, and tell me what was the most important thing you learned yesterday, and why? I will call on some of you in a few minutes to hear your responses.

Such a question is easy to conjure on a moment's notice and easy to deliver. Just as importantly, such a question buys valuable time for the teacher to get herself ready for the lesson.

DELIVERING QUESTIONS

The effective delivery of questions is an important skill for teachers to possess. Fortunately, there is a questioning strategy called GRAPPLE that can help teachers deliver questions strategically.

Origins of GRAPPLE

According to education consultant Gene Tavernetti, a South Carolina high school teacher introduced to him a mnemonic called APPLE, where A, P, P, L, and E stood for *ask a question, pause, pick a student, listen to the answer*, and *echo/elaborate/explain*, respectively.[1] (The name of the teacher appears lost to antiquity.) We will soon discuss each of these steps in detail.

Later, a West Coast professional development company added a T in front to form TAPPLE, where T stood for "teach first" (Hollingsworth and Ybarra, 2009, p. 22). Unfortunately, their "teach first" mandate assumes that teachers must explicitly teach content before they can question it, completely ignoring the fact that questions can prompt inquiry among students, therefore leading them on a search for answers. Such a narrow teacher-centered approach cannot accommodate such student-centered techniques as guided inquiry, which has risen in prominence since the Next Generation Science Standards took hold.

Because we strive to encompass both teacher- and student-centered instruction, we will revert to the original APPLE mnemonic but add a G to promote group-based learning and R to remind students of classroom rules on answering questions (and to form a cool word from the letters). See table 6.3.

Table 6.3 The GRAPPLE Mnemonic for Questioning Students.

Step	Activity
G	Group students strategically using DOK
R	Remind students of the questioning rules
A	Ask a question to the entire class multiple times
P	Pause to create adequate wait time using DOK
P	Pick a student strategically
L	Listen carefully to the student's answer
E	Effectively react to answers

Using GRAPPLE

Once teachers formulate a question in their minds (using the CPD), they can use GRAPPLE to deliver the question, as shown in table 6.3. We will now discuss each step of GRAPPLE, concentrating on the most significant departures from the TAPPLE method in Ref. (Hollingsworth and Ybarra 2009).

- Step G: Group students strategically using DOK

Research has shown that students learn more when allowed to discuss answers to questions in group settings (Petty 2006, Torbrand 2014). However, not all answers require group discussion. At the very outset, teachers should consider the cognitive complexity of their question to settle on whether they want students to ponder answers on their own, discuss possible answers with a peer (i.e., pair-share), or work in groups. Rather than form students into groups out of habit or gut feel, table 6.4 provides a strategy based on the DOK of the question. However, this table is just a baseline of suggestion. As professional decision-makers, teachers should make judgment calls based on their own experience (Olvera and Walkup 2010).

> My question aligns to DOK-2 more than anything else. The table suggests I use a pair-share to let students discuss possible answers. However, I know my students better than the evaluator sitting at the back of the room. I think letting them hash over answers in small groups will work better, especially for my English learners.

Table 6.4 illustrates how DOK impacts grouping strategies and wait time. We should note that Bloom's Taxonomy cannot serve as a replacement for DOK in the table. Simply put, Bloom's Taxonomy only identifies the *type* of thinking—not the *amount* of knowledge management—involved in formulating reasonable responses.

Table 6.4 Questioning Strategies for Student Grouping and Wait Time Based on Depth of Knowledge Levels

DOK Level	Grouping	Wait Time
DOK-1	Individual student	On the order of ten seconds
DOK-2	Pair-share	On the order of one minute
DOK-3	Informal groups	On the order of ten minutes
DOK-4	Formal groups*	Much longer than ten minutes

* Formal groups involve some form of structure, such as having one student act as recorder, another student acting as presenter, and so on.

To be clear, the strategies outlined in table 6.4 are not designed to differentiate instruction to individual students. This strategy assumes that all students in the classroom are responding to the same question and are therefore grouped similarly.

Note that nothing in this step suggests that teachers need to inform students how they plan to group them. Whether a teacher chooses to tell them now or a bit later depends on his or her personal style.

- Step R: Review the rules of questioning

The GRAPPLE questioning technique asks teachers to wait a predetermined time before calling on responses. When students first experience GRAPPLE, their inclination to belting out answers or raising their hands to answer questions can derail the best of questioning strategies. Therefore, it is a good idea to remind students of the rules of GRAPPLE.

> I am going to ask you a question about what we learned, but remember: Don't shout out the answer. Also, I will not be calling on raised hands, so don't bother raising them.

Even after being told to avoid shouting out answers, students will sometimes do so anyway. The best strategy probably is to not reward them with attention; over time, they will tend to quit such behavior.

- Step A: Ask the entire class the question multiple times

In this step, the teacher asks the questions to the whole class, and not just a single student. Repeating the question can help English Learners.

- Step P: Pause to create adequate wait time using DOK

We define wait time as the elapsed time between the moment teachers ask a question and the moment they request a response. Despite its benefits (Riley II 1986, Rowe 1987, Tobin 1987, Melder 2011), research shows that wait time is often too short (Swift and Gooding 1983, Tobin 1987, Rowe 1987, Duell et al. 1992, Baysen and Baysen 2010). There are many guidelines on what constitutes proper wait time, with the simplistic "at least three seconds" rule most predominant.

Rather than relying on one-size-fits all rules, we tie wait time to the DOK of the question. This makes sense, given that higher DOK levels involve more knowledge management. Table 6.4 shows that straightforward DOK-1 questions need the least wait time, as little as three seconds in some cases (Tobin 1980, Rowe 1987, Cotton 1988, Fletcher-Wood 2013). As DOK rises, the necessary wait time lengthens. By the time we reach DOK-4, our wait time might extend a full classroom period or even multiple classroom periods.

As professional decision-makers, teachers should not blindly follow guidelines. A DOK-2 question may require just 10 seconds; others may need more than two minutes. Struggling students often need more wait time than others. Increased wait time can benefit English Learners too, not only to formulate an answer but also to understand the nature of the question. Teachers should take into account all these considerations to adjust the guidelines in table 6.4 to suit their needs.

- Step P: Pick students strategically

Like everything else, the manner in which we select students should be strategic as well. The manner in which teachers select students to answer questions impacts the learning environment greatly. Separating questions into two types—checking for understanding and questioning for engagement—simplifies the strategy:

- Checking for understanding—teachers should employ mostly random sampling (e.g., equity sticks, playing cards).
- Questioning for engagement—teachers should employ the method of quasi-volunteers.

Referring back to its purpose, consider the following traditional, yet *ineffective*, methods of checking for understanding:

- The teacher asks, "Does everyone understand?" Whenever teachers expect students to communicate their own inadequacies, teachers will receive inadequate feedback. For one, many struggling students are too embarrassed to respond to such a question. Furthermore, informing the teacher of misunderstandings could cause the teacher to re-teach content (as it often should), much to the groans of classmates.[2]
- The teacher asks, "Does anyone have any questions?" There is nothing wrong with asking such a question once thorough checking for understanding has taken place. However, teachers should not confuse doing so with checking for understanding. By placing ourselves into the shoes of students, we can see the problem with this approach: asking questions when situated among peers is uncomfortable for many students. Worse, those experiencing the most discomfort are often those that struggle the most. Finally, students may not even know enough about the lesson to formulate a question.
- The teacher asks, "Who in here knows . . .?" Such questions shortchange students in two ways: (1) Apathetic students know that other students will likely raise their hands, allowing them to disengage. (2) Many who want to answer often get little chance, since "smarter kids" will always shoot their hands up before everyone else.

- Students shout answers. No questioning strategy negatively impacts the learning environment more than allowing students to blurt out answers unprompted. Besides its *zero wait time*, shout-outs prime students to misbehave throughout the entire day. At some point, shout-outs can evolve into a game, where students shout nonsense as part of the fun.

- Selecting students when checking for understanding

Stated again, checking for understanding refers to the practice of asking questions to monitor student understanding. In a sense, proper checking for understanding involves teachers performing a case study of their effectiveness throughout the lesson. For this reason, effective student selection adheres to acceptable statistical practices.

Researchers have found that certain groups of students talked more than three times as much as their classmates; a quarter of the students never participated at all. (Sadker and Sadker 1985) Many teachers engage only a select few students in the classroom to answer questions, while other students (usually the struggling and apathetic) tune out.

Ideally, when checking for understanding, we would like to retrieve answers from every student in the classroom. We can do so, but at some cost. For example, personal student whiteboards allow students to write answers and, in unison, show their answers to the teacher. An alternative is a clear sheet protector, with thick cardboard inserted between the sheets for rigidity. Although cheaper than hard whiteboards, sheet protectors require routine replacement.

For those that like high technology, digital student response systems (often called clickers) allow all students to submit answers in unison. Clickers also help teachers accumulate statistics on the individual performance of students (for use in intervention) and the class as a whole (for gauging teaching effectiveness). Since their introduction, clickers have become widespread, especially at the university level (Lee et al. 2011, Dallaire 2011). Despite their capabilities, the high cost of such systems may be out of reach for many K-12 schools.

Collecting feedback from an entire population is often out of bounds. In such situations, researchers resort to random sampling. Like social science researchers, we can (for the most part) measure teaching effectiveness and student understanding through random sampling by randomly calling on students to answer questions. The practice of random sampling (often called polling or cold calling) has formed a mainstay of K-12 professional development (Dallimore et al. 2004, Fisher and Frey 2007). University of Florida researcher Paige Allison is one of the few that has tested random sampling in controlled studies. As she puts it:

The interview data from the teachers and students shows this technique [random sampling of students] helped students do those things that we know help them to be successful in school—paying attention, being prepared for class, staying focused and doing homework. (Keen 2006)

Humans cannot select randomly. Deep in the backs of our minds, we tend to favor some numbers or call on certain students or areas of the classroom. Randomization tools ensure that student sampling follows reasonably random patterns. Equity sticks, which feature a student's name written on each stick (such as a Popsicle® stick), are the most common form of randomizer. Playing cards are preferred by many teachers because they are easy to carry and shuffle.[3]

On another note, although we strive to select students randomly, there may be students in the class that want to answer the question. Therefore, once the random sampling has ceased, we can ask for volunteers to offer their own responses. Post-polling volunteers can benefit student learning in other ways—quite often students have formulated responses that they are eager to share with their classmates. Such responses often provide useful insights into student learning.

- Selecting students when questioning for engagement

Unlike checking for understanding, questioning for engagement aims to boost student engagement. More often than not, questioning for engagement serves as a learning tool in of itself. With such questions, the time in which students haggle over potential answers provide the real learning moment, not so much the answer. This distinction in purpose impacts how we call on students, since the need to randomly poll students diminishes. Therefore, with questioning for engagement, we can select volunteers to answer questions while abiding the four principles of effective questioning we set out earlier in the chapter.

We must still find a way to accommodate all students in the learning environment. However, if students know that teachers will accept volunteers to answer questions, some will disengage. To remedy this situation, we resort to calling on *quasi-volunteers*. During the time when students discuss potential answers, this technique makes students think that their teacher will call on them at random to answer. A quasi-volunteer selection process looks like the following:

Teacher: I'm going to call on some of you at random to tell me which of these four causes of World War I was, in your opinion, the most important. So, get in your groups and discuss the four causes.
(Pause while students discuss responses)
Teacher: I'll tell you what . . . who in here wants to answer the question?

Notice that, in the end, the teacher called on volunteers to answer while still compelling students to engage the question meaningfully.

Step L: Listen carefully to student responses

See Hollingsworth and Ybarra (2009) for more discussion on this step.

Step E: Effectively react to students

Depending on whether the students' answers are correct, incorrect, or somewhere in between, teachers need to employ effective responses that further learning in the classroom and maintain student confidence. See Hollingsworth and Ybarra (2009) for more discussion.

HOMEWORK

Much debate on social media surrounds the issue of homework, with many calling on K-12 teachers to consider banning the assigning of homework. Colleges, however, demand considerable study skills, which revolve around the ability to ignore distractions in one's personal life and focus on carrying out assigned (and possibly dull) coursework when no one is looking.

But those opposed to homework have a point. Schools have increasingly ramped up the amount of homework students receive each night, usually out of a misguided notion that more homework means more learning. We can all appreciate the deleterious effects on student well-being that can arise from careless homework policies and practices. Consider the following:

> Although his biology project is due the next day, James has procrastinated for the last two hours. His assignment requires that he find and cite two books, two research articles, and a Web site. But James' family has no Internet access. The library is open, but he has no car and his mother is not due to come home from work until late. Besides, he has to stay home and watch over his little sister. (His father "split the scene" long ago.)
>
> James knows that he can complete a portion of the assignment and receive credit. But without the research, the best he can hope for is a C. Every time he starts working on the assignment, his mind wanders. "Why bother?" he asks himself. He knows that his teacher will chide him for not completing his project.
>
> He likes science and gets high grades on in-class tests, but his inability to complete science projects has eroded his confidence. To James, science is a chore.

The above vignette is fictitious, but not entirely unrealistic. Stories like James's getting played out all over the country every day. Obviously, addressing the barriers that James encounters poses a serious conundrum for educators.

The Problem with Banning Homework

By the very definition of homework, study skills cannot be simulated inside the classroom. The self-discipline needed to complete homework requires practice; anything assigned inside the classroom will fail to match the distractions that arise regularly at home. Furthermore, the very presence of a teacher in the classroom compels students to complete their tasks; at home, there is often no one around.

Consider now a district-wide ban on homework. After thirteen years of never having had to concentrate on coursework outside of the classroom, most students will stand little chance of meeting their college professor's expectations, especially in more rigorous majors.

In effect, banning homework widens the "life skills gap" in disadvantaged children, a problem that will remain hidden until their fourteenth year of instruction (when they enter college). Once entrenched, such a life-skills gap acts as a learning disability. Worse, this learning disability was not created by a biological phenomenon, but by the homework policy itself.

Students who live in cars will always be at a disadvantage, but banning homework places these kids at an even more severe disadvantage later in life. Teachers need a homework strategy that accommodates these students to the fullest extent possible while helping them develop the study habits needed for postsecondary success.

Before moving on, we need to exercise caution in placing too much stock in education research on the issue of homework. To determine whether homework benefits students, one needs to control for its quality. But that is rarely, if ever, done. Instead, all homework, including ridiculously severe homework loads and mindless drudgery, is lumped together in research studies. Nothing useful can be gleaned from such results.

Enter Depth of Knowledge

How can we assign homework and be fair to all kids? Norman Webb's DOK levels provide some guidelines. Visually scanning the definitions of each DOK level in chapter 1 demonstrates that activities aligned to higher levels require more external support, especially from peers. While students will likely not need any support for DOK-1 activities, DOK-4 will probably require full-blown formal group sessions. But the students we are discussing in this article do not have such support at home. Assigning homework activities that align to higher DOK levels isolates disadvantaged students.

Student Preparation

It does little good to assign homework students cannot complete because they lack the knowledge needed to carry out the problems. As education researchers Fisher and Frey argued in 2011, such homework tasks offer too many opportunities for students to learn things incorrectly, an unfortunate outcome since it takes so much time and effort to unlearn misconceptions and misunderstandings. (See "High-Quality Homework" by Frey and Fisher (2011) for more on this issue. For this reason, teachers should assess their students' ability to complete the homework they plan to assign. Those problems that are likely to disadvantage some students are best left for the classroom.

Take-Home Projects

Many of the traditional take-home projects that are commonplace in education are anathema to student learning. The typical bake-a-cell project (students bake a cake that looks like a biological cell, then decorate it with candies that represent organelles) is especially problematic; it teaches little but can place incredible stress on students coming from disadvantaged homes. Projects that require parents to purchase markers and trifold posters are equally problematic. Such projects may require parents to spend only $5 on supplies, but five bucks is a lot of money to some parents. (Furthermore, state laws may ban such a requirement outright.)

Faced with the task of telling their parents they will need to buy supplies for a project or will need their help to complete it, students procrastinate. In the end, they often tell their parents about the project the day before the deadline. The ensuing strife cannot possibly help the family environment.

Guidelines

Everyone has their own idea about the ideal homework load. Below are a few guidelines that could provide disadvantaged students some relief from misguided homework assignments while, at the same time, help students accumulate the study habits they will need later in life. As these serve as mere guidelines, they may be worth discussing with fellow teachers and school administrators.

1. The purpose of the assignment should be to practice that which has already been learned, so avoid assigning homework on concepts and skills that students have failed to learn proficiently.
2. Do not assign homework for students to learn new content. (Leave those assignments for the classroom.)

3. Stick to DOK-1 assignments that students can perform on their own; assign DOK-2 work only sparingly and never assign homework aligned to DOK-3 or DOK-4.
4. Students' time at home is valuable, so do not assign noncognitive take-home projects.
5. Keep the length of time needed to complete homework to reasonable levels. This may require teachers and administrators working as a team to account for student needs.
6. Never assign work that might require support from others, such as family members.
7. Never assign work that might require purchasing of materials by the student or family.
8. Never create a situation where failure to do homework impedes students' ability to succeed in the classroom.
9. Never assign homework as punishment.
10. Throw considerable effort into finding school-wide support for students who live in difficult environments.

Banning homework is a simplistic way to protect disadvantaged students from unfair homework loads, but pushes the "life-skills gap" into the college ranks, a complete contradiction to the notion of college preparedness. Rather than jump on the "Ban Homework!" bandwagon, we should think hard and deep to meet both the short-term and long-term needs of students.

SAMPLE LESSONS

Using table 6.2 we will now offer examples of questions that a teacher can use to check for understanding or questioning for engagement for each of the four sample lessons.

Sample Lesson A: Middle School ELA (Sports Journalism)

We can scan the Instructional Delivery Table in table 4.2 to identify some questions to check for understanding. Here are a few examples:

- How would you describe a metaphor in your own words?
- How would you describe figurative language in your own words?
- Is "She is nicer than my own grandmother," a metaphor? Explain.
- Why is it important to learn to write metaphors?
- How do you spell and pronounce metaphor?
- State the word metaphor in a sentence.

92   Chapter 6

To elevate the rigor of the lesson, we should also include some questions for engagement. Table 6.2 offers the following:

- Of the two metaphors you developed, which do you think strengthens your biography the most? Explain.
- Which step in creating a metaphor do you think is the hardest? Why?
- What qualities do you think are the most important in a metaphor?
- How would you describe the impact of your metaphors to your editor?
- Why do you think figurative language is used in music?
- Do you think metaphors belong in business communications? Why or why not?

Sample Lesson B: High School Art (Commercial Artist)

To check for understanding, we can ask the following:

- In your own words, what is the purpose of the principles of design?
- What does RFP stand for?
- What is the purpose of an RFP?
- What is the purpose of the terms of agreement?
- Why is it important to include a terms of agreement section in your proposal?
- Pick one of the principles of design you used in your sketch. Describe this principle of design in your own words.
- Do artists need to understand business principles? Explain.
- Name at least three terms that a terms of agreement should contain.

We can enliven discussion in the classroom and reinforce learning through the following questions:

- Pick one of the principles of design you used in your sketch. Describe the impact you think this principle of design had on the viewer.
- Why do you think the idea that artists need to understand business principles would be contentious among artists?
- Are there any terms in a terms of agreement that you think we have failed to discuss?

Sample Lesson C: High School Math (Cost Analyst)

To check for understanding, we can ask the following:

- Describe what is meant by the mean.
- Describe what is meant by the standard deviation.

- Describe what is meant by the standard error.
- What is the relationship between the standard deviation and standard error?
- Here is a set of mass measurements: 4.38, 4.44, 4.31, 4.37, 4.33. Draw box-and-whisker plots for this data.
- For the above measurements, predict confidence intervals for the population.
- What is the difference in how the standard deviation and standard error are used in statistics?
- What is the difference between a sample and a population?
- In class, we stated that the mean of the population will almost certainly reside within ±2SE of the sample mean. What do we mean by that?
- In class, we stated that the mean and standard deviation of a sample are only estimates of the population. What do we mean by that?

Some questions for engagement include:

- What are the three most important things you learned in this lesson?
- What part of this lesson are you most likely to forget and why?
- What would be the impact of a cost analyst ignoring confidence intervals?
- Write a short story that describes a business being impacted by the contents of today's lesson.

Sample Lesson D: Middle School Science (Quality Control Engineer)

To check for understanding, we can ask the following:

- Describe what is meant by proportional reasoning.
- How is density defined?
- What is the purpose of a box-and-whisker plot?
- Describe the structure of a box-and-whisker plot.
- Here is a set of mass measurements: 4.38, 4.44, 4.31, 4.37, 4.33. What is the mean, standard deviation, and standard error of this data set?
- How do you spell whisker?
- How do you spell and pronounce proportional?
- Use the word proportional in a sentence.
- What is the difference between a population and a sample?
- Describe the relationship between proportional reasoning and density.

Naturally, we can ask questions to raise engagement, such as the following:

- How would you describe the relationship between quality control and statistics?
- One of your local restaurants serves pizza that has lots of toppings on some days and relatively few toppings on other days. What are the possible

causes of this and what does each cause say about quality control in the restaurant?
- In class, we stated that high variation in measurements produces low confidence in measurement and that this low confidence could lead to large financial losses. Craft your own scenario of a business being affected by this condition.
- Why do you think it is important for a scientist to understand quality control? Explain.

NOTES

1. Personal correspondence, November 11, 2019.
2. Naturally, teachers should re-teach content if students have failed to learn it. In the case described here, however, a student's peers might blame the student for purposely slowing down instruction.
3. Teachers can write the names of students on the cards.

Chapter 7

Vignette

We have one more sample lesson to discuss, which will center on career-technical education. To highlight more of the process involved in lesson development, we will cast this sample lesson in the form of a vignette.

Sample Lesson E: High School CTE (Police Officer)

Sandy is a Nevada high school teacher that teaches in a juvenile justice pathway. Many of her students want to be police officers. Others want to be civil rights advocates or lawyers. Still others are in her course simply because none of the other electives interested them. Sandy wants to reach all of them in her next lesson.

Sandy turns to the lesson planning procedure in figure I.6 and begins to step through the process.

STEP 1

Sandy's course is guided by the Nevada CTE Criminal Justice Standards, which reflect one of many subcategories of the state's Health Science & Public Safety CTE standards (Office of Career Readiness 2019). She decides to select a standard that has risen in importance because of a recent upsurge in the sovereign citizen movement. Sovereign citizens belong to a sizable group of people who hold fringe views on rights and freedoms.

The Fourth Amendment is not only an important safeguard of individual liberties but also widely misunderstood. Because sovereign citizens tend to challenge police officers routinely on issues related to the Fourth Amendment, her lesson will address the issue directly. Performance Standard 2.3.4 states:

> Analyze the relevant case law concerning the Fourth Amendment.

She notes that the action verb is *analyze*, which ties directly to the *analyze* category of the CPD. Therefore, it will not be enough to merely *describe* the case law (the *understand* category of the CPD); her students will need to *dissect* the case law. As such, she expects that her lesson will require a wide range of instructional strategies.

Police officers are on the front lines in the civil rights debate and must have a thorough knowledge of the Fourth Amendment and how it restricts their powers to search property for illegal substances. Her students will examine what a police officer can and cannot do in conducting a traffic stop. A central focus of the lesson will be the higher purposes of the Fourth Amendment in terms of preserving rights and freedoms weighed against the challenges of keeping our streets safe through criminal investigation. Sandy wants her students to explore this balance guided by a culminating activity.

STEP 2

Police officers face conflict all the time. Such conflicts often arise when one or both parties misunderstand constitutional rights. Sandy decides that conflict is a good vehicle for getting students engaged in her lesson, for which she can use the conflict resolution template from chapter 2.

> You are working as a [job title] when a dispute over [issue] surfaces.

Wanting her students to aim high in their future careers, Sandy decides to use Police Chief for the job title, which will help elevate the responsibility of their role and therefore DOK of the lesson. The dispute is clear—under which conditions is a search legal? Sandy settles on the culminating activity:

> You are a police chief whose officers have constantly wrangled with sovereign citizens over vehicle searches. To train your officers on handling such situations, you have decided to write a point/counterpoint script that looks at civil rights from the perspective of both the motorist and the officer. Working as a team, you will act out the script on video as part of an online training program.

A point/counterpoint script will require considerable digestion of information regarding the U.S. Constitution, case law, and statutes. More importantly, such a script will require her students to view the issue from both sides of the coin. Because the starting point for the activity requires some brainstorming, the final output is not dictated, and there is considerable decision-making involved, this activity most closely aligns with DOK-4, as indicated in table I.2. As such, formal groups would be a good vehicle for group collaboration.

For a learning objective, Sandy decides on the following:

> Today, we will analyze the Fourth Amendment as it pertains to searches of a vehicle during a traffic stop.

Because her students will have to write a point/counterpoint script and deliver it verbally in the classroom, this lesson will incorporate the language objectives of writing and speaking.

> Today, you will write a script and deliver it verbally.

STEP 3

Sandy has now established a culminating activity for her lesson. For her step, she needs to outline the content of her lesson.

Sandy's lesson plan focuses on the issue of searching vehicles at a traffic stop. The level of knowledge attainment targets that which we would expect of a police officer, not a lawyer or judge. Still, she will find that such a seemingly straightforward case involves ample complexity.

For this lesson, she uses the expanded KD to select the lesson content. She asks herself, "What do I want my students to always *remember* from the lesson?" She reflects back on the most important facts that a police officer would need to remember to make good decisions when it comes to searching vehicles.

For one, the officer needs to *remember* that the Fourth Amendment is designed to protect us from unreasonable searches and seizures. Also, many sovereign citizens rely on overly literal interpretations of constitutional rights, so the officer needs to *remember* that states pass laws that can affect how the Fourth Amendment affects the police's ability to inspect property. But he also needs to *remember* that appeals courts decide whether those laws violate the Fourth Amendment and that these appeals court decisions in turn become law *(case law* or *common law)*.

Finally, the officer needs to *remember* that he can only search a car if he has *probable cause* and that *probable cause* is defined as "a reasonable amount of suspicion, supported by circumstances sufficiently strong to justify a prudent and cautious person's belief that certain facts are probably true" (Handler 1994). Ideally, the officer should have this definition *memorized*.

Sandy next thinks about conceptual knowledge. She asks herself, "What do I need my students to always *understand*?" First, students should be able to *interpret* the Fourth Amendment and describe it in their own words. Although, it would be ideal if the officer has *memorized* the definition of probable cause, it will do little good unless he *understands* it. However, the term "probable cause" is often confused with *reasonable suspicion* and *reasonable doubt*, so students will need to *understand* these terms and be able to *distinguish* between them. Finally, she thinks it is a good idea for her students to *understand* what is meant by the term "sovereign citizen."

Next, Sandy asks herself "What do I want my students to be able to *do*?" This lesson centers on *writing* a point/counterpoint script on whether it is permissible for police to search a vehicle, so she wants to helps students develop the skill in *writing* point/counterpoint scripts, which she knows also satisfies a language objective. To do this, however, they will need to learn how to *search* and *find* relevant case law with respect to vehicle searches. Both skills will involve ample critical thinking.

As a seasoned teacher, Sandy knows the importance of helping students build metacognitive knowledge. One way for students to gauge their own understanding of the Fourth Amendment surrounding vehicle searches is for them to *conjure* exceptional circumstances for which they do not know the answer. They can then *list* such questions and *identify* strategies for exploring answers to them in the future. When reading lesson content, Sandy plans to have her students *log* their emotions and confidence according to whether they understand the lesson or find the lesson confusing.

The next question Sandy ponders is "Why would my students care to learn this lesson?" After thinking it over and scanning the Relevance Taxonomy Table in chapter 2, she arrives at a number of reasons. First, there is personal/future relevance. Even those students who have no plans of being a police chief may find the lesson valuable—by *understanding* their rights, they can avoid unreasonable searches.

Along the same lines, those wanting to be police officers will routinely pull motorists over for traffic stops, and so they need to *understand* under which conditions they can search a vehicle. If they do it wrong, they could end up forcing a district attorney to drop charges against someone who may have committed a serious crime.

There is also scholarly/academic relevance. The term "probable cause" is commonly used but also not always understood. Citizens are expected, to some degree, to be learned in the legal profession.

Sandy also wants to build communicative knowledge in her students. Sandy knows that collaboration is an important skill to build for all students, so for her lesson she will have students *work* in formal groups to examine the issue of vehicle searches from both the officer's and motorist's point of view. They will then *create* the point/counterpoint script and present it to the class, with each student *acting* out one of the script roles.

To chunk the speaking skills, she decides to focus only on clarity and voice inflections for this lesson. She will ask students to (1) select a few words in their statements that they will emphasize with effective voice inflections of their choosing and (2) practice enunciating their statements prior to delivery. Finally, Sandy wants to *build* vocabulary skills in her students and selects the terms "sovereign" and "citizen," paying special attention to the spelling and pronunciation of sovereign.

Sandy next turns to the question, "What background knowledge am I naively assuming they have that they might not?" Looking over her Lesson Content Table, she spots a few areas of potential struggle.

- Some students have little experience in public speaking, or are exceptionally nervous speaking in public, or both.
- This lesson centers on writing a point/counterpoint script, which typically targets sentence-level writing skills. However, not all students come to the table with adequate writing skills.

STEP 4

Now that Sandy knows *what* to teach, she needs to identify strategies for *how* to teach it. For that, she decides to create an Instructional Delivery Table. By looking over the (italicized) action verbs in the Lecture Content Table for her lesson, she picks a few strategies for each CPD.

How does she make these choices? Cognitive strategies are fundamental to instruction and effective for teaching recall, so picking them to teach academic content targeting the *remember* category of the CDP is to her a no-brainer. For example, she can declare that "states pass laws that affect how the 4th Amendment affects the police's ability to inspect property," then have students write this fact in their notebooks as reinforcement.

To help students understand such statements, Sandy turns to the elaboration cognitive strategy. She elaborates on the meaning of such statements and provides examples of how states have passed such laws in the past and how more recent decisions have relied on these prior court decisions when rendering judgment. She thinks showing an entertaining clip of a sovereign citizen forgetting this fact will reinforce comprehension even more.

Sandy is well versed in the Socratic method and wants to continue using it to develop this skill set. She decides to start out with a prompt to get conversation flowing:

An officer has pulled a motorist over and thinks that he sees illegal substances in the car. He plans to search the car. Can he?

In preparation for the Socratic seminar, Sandy prepares a number of prompts to get students questioning their own understanding of the law, including:

- What if the substance turns out to be merely sugar? Do you think he has violated the motorist's rights? Explain.
- What if the person is a known past offender? Should that help him establish probable cause? Explain.
- What if the person is acting like he is impaired? Should that help the officer establish probable cause? Explain.
- Suppose the passenger tells the officer that he *thinks* there could be drugs in the car. Should that help him establish probable cause? Explain.
- What if the officer thinks he smells marijuana? Should that help him establish probable cause? Explain.

Throughout the Socratic seminar, Sandy plans to emphasize what students think should be essential for probable cause and not worry about whether their understanding is factual. She knows that later she will fill them in on relevant facts from case law so that none of her students leave the classroom with misconceptions.

To teach students to collaborate effectively, Sandy employs the Team Learning model developed at the University of Oklahoma, which she uses for all her formal group sessions (Michaelsen et al. 2001).

She then needs to think about background barriers and what to do about them. She knows that a couple of her students are a bit frightened to speak publicly, but she reminds herself that the public speaking part of this lesson focuses purely on clarity and effective voice inflections in speech. She decides to limit these students' involvement to just one or two statements. If they falter, she figures that she can ask them to try again privately after the lesson is over to see if they can enunciate their statements properly.

She also notes that some students struggle with writing at the sentence level. However, sentence-level grammar does not constitute any part of the expanded KD, so Sandy knows she is free to support students as much as she wants in crafting proper sentences.

In the end, Sandy's Instructional Delivery Table looks like the one in table 7.1.

Table 7.1 Sandy's Instructional Delivery Table for Sample Lesson E

Category	Students will . . .	Technique
Remember	*remember* the Fourth Amendment protects from unreasonable searches/seizures	Rehearsal
	remember that states pass laws that affect how the Fourth Amendment affects the police's ability to inspect, property	Rehearsal
	remember that appeals courts decide whether those laws violate the Fourth Amendment	Rehearsal
	remember that appeals court decisions become law (case/common law)	Rehearsal
	remember that probable cause is needed to search a vehicle	Rehearsal
	recall the definition of probable cause	Rehearsal
Understand	*interpret* the Fourth Amendment	Elaboration
	understand probable cause, reasonable suspicion, and proof beyond reasonable doubt	Elaboration
	distinguish between probable cause, reasonable suspicion, and proof beyond reasonable doubt	Elaboration
	understand the term "sovereign citizen"	Elaboration
	understand that the knowledge of Fourth Amendment helps avoid conflict	Elaboration
	understand that the knowledge of Fourth Amendment helps protect rights	Elaboration
Apply	*exhibit* clarity and effective voice inflections in speech	Coaching
	spell and *pronounce* sovereign and citizen	Rehearsal
	work in formal groups	Team Learning
Analyze	*analyze* the conditions under which a car can be searched	Socratic seminar
Evaluate	*assess* their own understanding of the Fourth Amendment	Socratic seminar
	log emotions/confidence according to whether they understand the lesson	Metacog Log
	list questions they could use to explore the topic in the future	
	evaluate their confidence in interpreting a person's Fourth Amendment rights	Metacog Log
Create	*write* point/counterpoint script on whether it is permissible to search vehicle	Elaboration
	BACKGROUND BARRIERS	
Apply	*speak* publicly	Private coaching
	writing at the sentence level	Private coaching

STEP 5

Checking for Understanding

Sandy understands the importance of sprinkling her lesson with questions that will help her determine whether her lesson has been effective. One question at the DOK-2 level strikes at the heart of the matter:

- Describe the difference between *probable cause* and *reasonable suspicion*.

She uses the GRAPPLE method of questioning students.

Students, I am going to ask you to pair-share for this next question. Again, do not blurt out answers. "How would you describe the difference between probable cause and reasonable suspicion to a friend who doesn't know much about the law? Probable cause . . . reasonable suspicion . . . how would you tell your friend how they differ?" Okay, talk to your partner.

After about thirty seconds, Sandy pulls a name from her deck of cards. "Samantha, how would you describe the difference between probable cause and reasonable suspicion?"

After questioning at least two more students, Sandy asks the class "Do any of you have some responses that you want to offer?"

Other questions/prompts that Sandy formulates to check for understanding include:

- What is meant by case law?
- Under which conditions can a car be searched by a police officer?
- State one element of the Fourth Amendment.
- How would you describe a sovereign citizen?

Questioning for Engagement

Sandy knows that when questioning for engagement, she can call on volunteers to respond to her questions or prompts. She also knows that making students think she will call on them randomly will prompt them to work extra hard to formulate adequate responses.

For this next question, I am going to have you team up in threes. As a reminder, do not blurt out answers . . . I will call on three students randomly, so be prepared. Okay, here is the question, "Are there any exceptions to the probable cause requirement that you think should apply?"

As a DOK-2 question, Sandy gives students ample time in pair-shares to formulate an answer. She then states, "Rather than pick on one of you to answer, do any of you have any suggestions?"

Other questions/prompts Sandy formulates to engage students include:

- Why is the Fourth Amendment important?
- Why do you think it is important for *you* to understand the Fourth Amendment?
- List five things you consider the most important to remember from this lesson in their order of importance.
- Describe one important aspect of today's lesson that you want to explore further.

DELIVERY ORDER

To deliver the lesson in table 7.1, Sandy decides to start off with the *analyze* category of the CDP, using a Socratic seminar to highlight the relevant issues and spur interest in the subject. (This infuses a light form of discovery learning in the lesson.) Once finished, she thinks it is best to address the content in the *remember* and *understand* categories, using a mix of rehearsal and elaboration cognitive strategies to instill long-term memory and comprehension. All the while, students will monitor their own learning while Sandy continually checks for understanding and questions for engagement.

After a series of checking for understanding indicates that students mostly learned the lesson, students work in formal groups to prepare their point/counterpoint scripts, for which they plan to deliver in class the next day.

HOMEWORK

For homework, Sandy decides to assign a few DOK-1 and DOK-2 questions to ease the demand for peer/parental support and mitigate the homework time load. She settles on the following:

1. In your own words, describe the Fourth Amendment.
2. In your own words, describe why the Fourth Amendment is important for citizens.
3. In your own words, summarize why the Fourth Amendment is a cause for conflict.

Sandy wants students to think about the lesson further, so she also assigns the following:

4. If as a police officer you pull someone over for speeding, under what circumstances do you think you should be able to search the car? Justify your answer.

Sandy knows that students won't need any technology or parental help to simply ponder the problem and formulate some responses. Such a question will get them critically reflecting on what they learned in class, an effective way to reinforce recall of the content.

Sandy's district has issued guidelines for homework, which stipulate that the total daily homework load for a high school freshman remain below 90 minutes. Sandy surmises that this assignment would only take about twenty minutes to complete. Given that students also have homework in their other classes, this seems to be a reasonable homework burden.

Appendix A

Instructional Strategies

The number of instructional strategies available to teachers is vast. The following strategies are some of the most common and are used in the sample lesson plans in this book. Out of concerns for brevity, we can only describe these strategies to a modest level.

COGNITIVE STRATEGIES

How can we teach students to *remember*? The rehearsal cognitive strategy is an effective method for shifting lesson content into students' long-term memories. Cognitive strategies are internal skills that can help students remember and think as they learn new content (Gagne and Briggs 1979, p. 71). Besides the rehearsal cognitive strategy, we can include elaboration and organization strategies (Weinstein and Mayer 1986), which we will also leverage for teaching certain content. Cognitive strategies are a mainstay of most direct instruction methods such as the Instructional Theory into Practice model by Madeline Hunter (1995).

With the rehearsal strategy, students learn through repetition. At its most basic level, asking students to repeat something aloud multiple times or copy content into their notebooks falls into this category. Some common rehearsal techniques include memorizing, loud reading, listing concepts, and taking notes (Simsek and Balaban 2010, Pressley and Harris 2017). The choral response, where the class utters a statement in unison, is another example. Chunking, where we split content into smaller parts easier to memorize, is another cognitive strategy. An example of chunking is our phone number, which chunks the area code, exchange, and line number to make it easier to remember. Other chunking strategies include highlighting and underlining.

Students can rehearse content all week, but will they understand what they have memorized? To reinforce the *understand* category of the CPD, we can use the cognitive strategy called *elaboration*. Examples, counterexamples, and analogies form three of the most important elaboration techniques. For example, to teach students to understand parallelism in writing we can provide examples and counterexamples, explaining the reasoning behind our choices. Drawing analogies between the solar system (something familiar) and the structure of an atom (one of the lesson concepts) could help clarify student understanding of atomic orbitals.

Organizational cognitive strategies help students organize content. For example, consider the mnemonic device ROYGBIV, which stands for red, orange, yellow, green, blue, indigo, and violet. The linguistic appeal of this device makes it easy to remember not just the colors that appear in the visible spectrum but also the order in which they appear (the frequency of each color ascends to the right, so orange is of higher frequency than red, yellow is of higher frequency than orange, and so on. Graphic organizers and logic models are also examples of important organizational cognitive strategies used for writing essays and other multi-section manuscripts; they should form a standard feature of writing instruction.

GRADUAL RELEASE OF RESPONSIBILITY (GRR)

The GRR method of Pearson and Gallagher (1983) often works well for teaching *apply*-, *analyze*-, *evaluate*-, and *create*-level thinking. This method involves four stages, as shown in figure A.1 (Fisher 2008, Webb et al. 2019).

- During the *Focus Learning phase*, the teacher (T) controls content delivery, relying on direct instruction skills, cognitive strategies, and questioning strategies to teach students (S) the background knowledge needed to begin. (Here, the letters A–G in the figure represents distinct tasks.)
- During the *Guided Instruction phase*, the teacher groups students into homogeneous (based on need) informal groups, working on a common task chosen for its alignment to their needs (i.e., differentiation). During this phase, however, the teacher retains control of the learning.
- During *Collaborative Learning*, students form into heterogeneous groups and work on their own tasks while supporting each while the teacher monitors and facilitates the discussion.
- Finally, in the *Independent Tasks* phase, students work on their own tasks while the teacher provides minimal support.

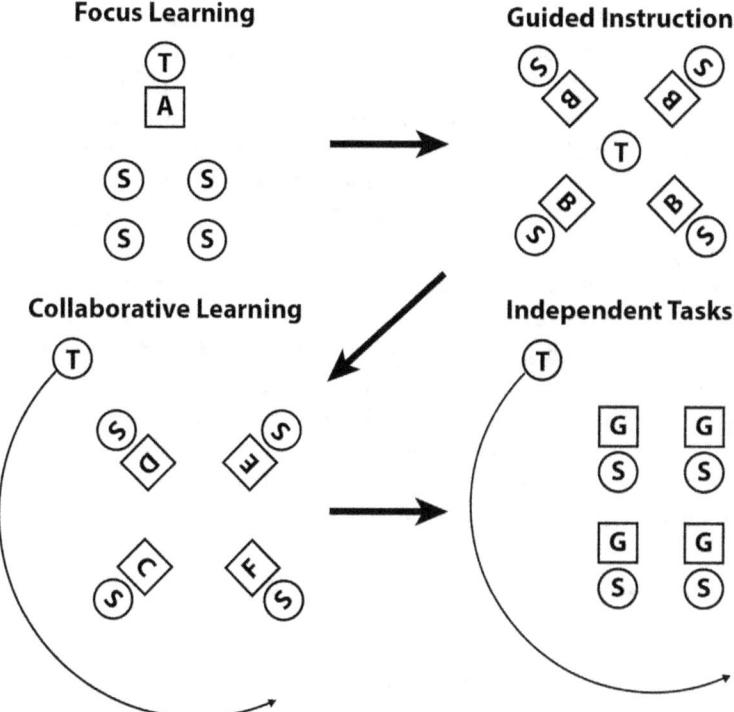

Figure A.1 A Visual Representation of the Gradual Release of Responsibility Model. Here, S and T stand for the student and teacher, respectively, and A–G stand for individual tasks. *Source*: Author.

I DO, WE DO, YOU DO

Often confused with GRR (which has four steps), I Do, We Do, You Do is less complex. When teaching content targeted for this method, the teacher at first assumes the dominant role in lesson delivery (i.e., the *I Do* phase), with the teacher usually relying on tried-and-true direct instruction strategies such as rehearsal, elaborating, modeling, and questioning. Once teachers feel that their students have understood the content, they shift the responsibility more onto students by having them contribute a step in the lesson plan under their teacher's guidance (i.e., the *We Do* phase). Finally, in the *You Do* phase, students are asked to perform independently (Levy 2008, Ginsburg 2015).

For a simple example, consider a lesson in which a teacher is teaching students to identify active and passive sentences. Here, the teacher uses the Think-Aloud in the I Do phase:

- *I Do:* The first thing I'm going to do in this sentence "The dog bit the man" is circle the subject—the dog—and underline the action verb. That will help me make decisions on whether the subject performs the action. Now let's see, does the subject perform the action? Hmmm yes! The dog is the subject and the dog did the biting. Let me think, when the subject does the action, that's the passive voice. (Note that the think aloud should be followed by rigorous questioning. We have omitted the questioning for brevity.)
- We Do: Now, let's do one together. Remember, the subject of the sentence is what the sentence is about. Can you circle the subject in the sentence "This part was made by Bob"? Now, the action is a verb that describes what is going on. Can you underline the verb? Now, is the part doing the making? Correct, the answer is no. So, is this sentence active or passive? Yes, you are right. This sentence is passive.
- You Do: Consider the sentence "The tree fell down by the road." On your own, identify this sentence as passive or active.

Additional examples can be found in Ginsburg (2015).

THINK-ALOUDS

As shown in figure A.2, the think-aloud is often an effective vehicle for teaching students across a wide range of CPD categories, especially in reading instruction (Gold and Gibson 2001, Farr and Conner 2004). According to author Jeffrey Wilhelm (2001), "Think-alouds make invisible mental processes visible to children."

The think-aloud involves the verbalizing of one's own thought processes as he or she tackles complex tasks (van Someren 1994, Conrady 2015). As such,

Figure A.2 The Think-Aloud Involves Transforming One's Inner Thought Processes into Verbal Statements. *Source*: Author.

think-alouds are always cast in the first-person singular. One simple way to understand the think-aloud is to transform the "thought bubble" in a cartoon to a "speech bubble" as shown in figure A.2. The idea is that by hearing the teacher's thought process, students will acquire such thinking strategies gradually. In this sense, the think-aloud teaches students to think by example.

Here, we can offer again the sample metaphor "Winston Churchill was the bulldog of the pack," and verbalize out loud our thought processes as we *evaluate* the effectiveness of the metaphor:

> Hmmm . . . one thing I want to accomplish is to spice up my writing using figurative language. The first metaphor I used was "Winston Churchill was the bulldog of the pack." I know that Winston Churchill is the tenor, because he is the man we are trying to describe with a metaphor. I chose a bulldog for the vehicle because, like Churchill, the bulldog is short and squat and has a grumpy, dour face. Also, the bulldog is a popular symbol of England, so that works, too. I also like the fact that I used the term "pack" to describe the meeting participants, which is also a metaphor. There is one thing I don't like—the bulldog may be short and mean, but is it a leader among dogs? Hmmm . . . I'm not so sure. Also, Churchill is compared to a bulldog a lot. Am I being really creative? Maybe this isn't the best metaphor to use after all. I'm going to have to rethink this one.

The think-aloud is typically a pencils-down activity, with students listening intently rather than taking notes. Checking for understanding and questioning for engagement questions should follow each think-aloud to compel students to focus on the teacher's thought processes. For the example shown above, we could ask students questions such as "What did I consider when I judged the quality of my metaphor?" and "What else do you think I could have considered?"

SOCRATIC SEMINARS

As indicated in figure 4.2, Socratic seminars often work well for teaching students to *understand, analyze,* or *evaluate* complex issues. The Socratic method is a process used to engage information in the form of a dialect between teacher and students (Wilberding 2019). The name derives from Socrates's teaching method, where he feigned ignorance about some topic to force his students to draw out of him all he knew about the topic. By continually confronting students with hypothetical situations that illuminated errors in their preconceived notions, Socrates was able to guide students toward more acceptable ideas.

The following is an example of a Socratic session focused on the legality of personal searches of students' property:

Teacher: "Is it right for a school resource officer to search your backpack?"
Student 1: "No"
Student 2: "Well, if the student has a bomb or drugs in his backpack."
Teacher: "So would it be ok to search backpacks off campus if officers believe students have a weapon or drugs?"
Student 4: "No"
Teacher: "Why? What is the difference between a student having a weapon or drugs on campus versus off campus?"
Student 5: "On campus other students are at risk and a cop's job is to keep students safe."
Teacher: "Well, couldn't students off campus also be in danger?"
Student 6: "Yes, it's just different when they're off campus than when they're on campus."
Teacher: "Alright, it appears that we have much to consider."

By participating in this example of the Socratic method, teachers can guide students to reach evidenced-backed conclusions while deepening their knowledge of a complex topic. All of these factors will reinforce her students' understanding of the Fourth Amendment.

One advantage of the Socratic method is that it compels students to ponder opposing viewpoints, rather than arguing from only their own preferred personal angle. Once completed, students can summarize their discussions in the form of a point/counterpoint script, which further intensifies the need to bend over backward to see issues from a different personal lens.

Those interested in learning more about implementing the Socratic method in their classrooms should consider reading *The Power of the Socratic Classroom* by Charles Ames Fischer (2019), *Socratic Circles: Fostering Critical and Creative Thinking in Middle and High School* by Matt Copeland (2010) and *Socratic Methods* by Wilberding (2019).

GUIDED INQUIRY

Guided inquiry is a good candidate for teaching students to think at the *understand*, *apply*, and *analyze* CPD categories. One method used to lead students through a guided inquiry session is the 5E model developed by BSCS Science Learning, which comprises five steps: (Bybee et al. 2006, Molebash et al. 2019, Wolfe 2019)

- *Engagement*—connect past and present learning experiences, expose prior conceptions, and organize students' thinking toward the learning outcomes of current activities.

- *Exploration*—assign lab activities that help students use prior knowledge to generate new ideas, explore questions and possibilities, and design and conduct a preliminary investigation.
- *Explanation*—focus students' attention on a particular aspect of their engagement and exploration experiences and provide them opportunities to demonstrate their conceptual understanding, process skills, or behaviors.
- *Elaboration*—challenge and extend students' conceptual understanding and skills through additional activities that compel students to apply their understanding of the concept.
- *Evaluation*—encourage students to assess their understanding and abilities and provide opportunities to evaluate their progress toward achieving the educational objectives.

Guided inquiry is not just for science teachers. Sample Lesson C illustrates how the 5E method can drive guided inquiry for teaching an art lesson on sculpture.

METACOGNITION QUESTION BANK

A number of online resources post questions that teachers can have students ask themselves to promote metacognition (McGaan 2015, Chick 2018). For example, Lisa Chesser (2014) contributed fifty such questions to TeachThought.com, which fall into seven major categories:

1. Reflection & Collaboration (e.g., "What do you think about what was said? How would you agree or disagree with this?")
2. Self-Reflection (e.g., "Why does that answer make sense to you? Why didn't you consider a different route to the problem?")
3. Reasoning (e.g., "How might you argue against this? How do you think this is true?")
4. Analysis (e.g., "How might you show the differences and similarities? What patterns might lead you to an alternative answer?")
5. Connections (e.g., How does this relate daily occurrences? Which ideas make the most sense and why?")
6. Literary Questions (e.g., "What surprised or confused you about the characters or events? Explain. How did the character's actions affect you? Explain.")
7. Science and Social Questions (e.g., "What concepts help organize this data, or these experiences? Which set of data or information is most relevant or important?")

	Metacog Log		
	What makes sense	What I find confusing	Emoji
Part 1			 😀 😉 😟 😐 😲 😯 😨 😠
Part 2			 😀 😉 😟 😐 😲 😯 😨 😠
Part 3			 😀 😉 😟 😐 😲 😯 😨 😠

Figure A.3 Metacog Log metacognition monitor for Students to Log Their Thought Processes Throughout Each Part of a Lesson. *Source*: Author.

METACOG LOG

Students can use the Metacog Log in figure A.3 to self-assess their own proficiency by commenting on their triumphs and struggles, as well as circling the emoji that summarizes their emotions toward the content. Teachers can scan the table as students work on projects to uncover areas of struggle. For more complex activities, new rows can be added to reflect individual phases of the project.

Appendix B

Templates

To develop lesson plans, teachers can use the templates in table B.1 and table B.2.

Table B.1 Template for Developing a Lesson Content Table.

Component	Students will . . .
Grade-Appropriate Content	
Factual	
Conceptual	
Procedural	
Metacognitive	
Relevance	
Communicative	
Background Barriers	
Factual	
Conceptual	
Procedural	

Appendix B

Table B.2 Template for Building an Instructional Delivery Table

Category	Students will . . .	Technique
Grade-Appropriate Content		
Remember		
Understand		
Apply		
Analyze		
Evaluate		
Create		
Background Barriers		
Remember		
Understand		
Apply		

References

Albergaria-Almeida, Patricia. 2012. "Classroom questioning: Teacher's perceptions and practices." *Procedia – Social and Behavioral Sciences* 31: 634–638. https://doi.org/10.1016/j.sbspro.2011.12.116.

Anderson, L. W. (Ed.), D. R. Krathwohl (Ed.), P. W. Airasian, K. A. Cruikshank, R. E. Mayer, P. R. Pintrich, J. Raths, and M. C. Wittrock. 2001. *A Taxonomy for Learning, Teaching, and Assessing: A Revision of Bloom's Taxonomy of Educational Objectives*. New York City, NY: Longman.

Baysen, Engin, and Fatma Baysen. 2010. "Prospective teachers' wait-times." *Procedia Social and Behavioral Sciences* 2: 5172–5176. https://doi:10.1016/j.sbspro.2010.03.841.

Beane, J. 2001. "Rigor and relevance: Can we have our cake and eat it too?" Paper presented at the Annual Conference of the National Middle School Association, Washington DC.

Black, Paul, and Dylan Wiliam. 2001. "Inside the black box: Raising standards through classroom assessment." White paper, London School of Education, King's College, London. https://weaeducation.typepad.co.uk/files/blackbox-1.pdf.

Blackburn, Barbara R. 2008. *Rigor is Not a Four-letter Word*. Larchmont, NY: Routledge Eye on Education.

Blackburn, Barbara R., and Ronald Williamson. 2009. "The characteristics of a rigorous classroom." *Instructional Leader* 22 (6): 1–3. http://static.pdesas.org/content/documents/M4-Slide_11_Characteristics_of_a_Rigorous_Classroom.pdf.

Bloom, B. S., M. D. Engelhart, E. J. Furst, W. H. Hill, and D. R. Krathwohl. 1956. *Taxonomy of Educational Objectives: The Classification of Educational Goals Handbook I: Cognitive Domain*. New York, NY: David McKay Company.

Bogess, J. A. 2007. "The three Rs redefined for a flat world." *Techniques: Connecting Education & Careers* 82: 62.

Buck Institute of Education. 2019. "What is PBL?" March 7. https://www.pblworks.org/what-is-pbl.

References

Bybee, Rodger W., Joseph A. Taylor, April Gardner, Pamela Van Scotter, Janet Carlson Powell, Anne Westbrook, and Nancy Landes. 2006. "The BSCS 5E instructional model: Origins and effectiveness." Colorado Springs, CO: BSCS. Accessed April 5, 2019. https://media.bscs.org/bscsmw/5es/bscs_5e_full_report.pdf.

Carlson, A. 2017. "The effect of implementing Hess' Cognitive Rigor Matrix within fifth-grade independent learning-contracts upon student engagement and time-on-task." Master's Thesis. St. Catherine University. Accessed April 4, 2019. https://sophia.stkate.edu/maed/289.

Chesser, Lisa. 2014. "Student-driven learning: 50 challenging questions to ask your students." InformED. May 26. https://www.opencolleges.edu.au/informed/features/student-driven-learning/.

Chick, Nancy. 2018. "Metacognition: Thinking about one's thinking." Accessed May 22, 2019. https://cft.vanderbilt.edu/guides-sub-pages/metacognition/.

Clark, Ruth C., and Chopeta Lyons. 2004. *Graphics for Learning: Proven Guidelines for Planning, Designing, and Evaluating Visuals in Training Materials*. Jossey-Bass/Pfeiffer.

Clark, Ruth C., and Richard E. Mayer. 2007. *E-Learning and the Science of Instruction: Proven Guidelines for Consumers and Designers of Multimedia Learning*. San Francisco, CA: Pfeiffer.

Colorado Professional Learning Network. 2012. "Depth-of-Knowledge in the fine arts." February 26. https://www.coloradoplc.org/files/archives/dok-arts.pdf.

Common Core State Standards Initiative. 2010. *Common Core Standards for English Language Arts & Literacy in History/Social Studies, Science, and Technical Subjects*. Washington, DC: National Governors Association Center for Best Practices & Council of Chief State School Officers.

Conrady, Kansas. 2015. "Modeling metacognition: Making thinking visible in a content course for teachers." *REDIMAT* 4 (2): 132–160. http://dx.doi.org/10.17583/redimat.2015.1422.

Copeland, Matthew. 2010. *Socratic Circles: Fostering Critical and Creative Thinking in Middle and High School*. Portland, MN: Stenhouse.

Cotton, Kathleen. 1988. "Classroom questioning." Portland, OR: North West Regional Educational Laboratory. https://educationnorthwest.org/sites/default/files/classroom-questioning.pdf.

Dallaire, Danielle H. 2011. "Effective use of personal response 'Clicker' systems in psychology courses." *Teaching of Psychology* 38 (3): 199–204. https://doi.org/10.1177/0098628311411898.

Dallimore, Elise J., Julie H. Hertenstein, and Marjorie B. Platt. 2004. "Classroom participation and discussion effectiveness: Student-generated strategies." *Communication Education* 53 (1): 1.

Duell, O., D. Lynch, R. Ellsworth, and C. Moore. 1992. "Wait-time in college classes taken by education majors." *Research in Higher Education* 33 (4): 483–495.

Eberly Center at Carnegie Mellon University. 2019. "What is the difference between formative and summative assessment?" https://www.cmu.edu/teaching/assessment/basics/formative-summative.html.

Echevarria, Jane, Mary Ellen Vogt, and Deborah J. Short. 2008. *Making Content Comprehensible to English Learners: The SIOP Model*. Boston: Allyn & Bacon.

Farr, Roger, and J. Jenny Conner. 2014. "Using think-alouds to improve reading comprehension." Accessed August 30, 2018. http://www.ldonline.org/article/102.

Fischer, Charles Ames. 2019. "The Socratic circle." Accessed April 11, 2019. https://www.corndancer.com/tunes/tunes_print/soccirc.pdf.

Fisher, Douglas. 2008. *Effective Use of the Gradual Release of Responsibility Model*. McGraw Hill Education.

Fisher, Douglas, and Nancy Frey. 2014. *Checking for Understanding: Formative Assessment Techniques for Your Classroom*. 2nd Ed. Alexandria, VA: ASCD.

Fletcher-Wood, Harry. 2013. "Before you say anything – count to three." August 17. Accessed August 10, 2019. https://improvingteaching.co.uk/2013/08/17/increasing-wait-time/.

Francis, Erik. 2016. *Now That's a Good Question! How to Promote Cognitive Rigor Through Classroom Questioning*. Alexandria, VA: ASCD.

Frey, Nancy, and Douglas Fisher. 2011. "High-quality homework." *Instructional Leader*: 12 (2): 56–58.

Gagne, R. M., and L. J. Briggs. 1979. *Principles of Instructional Design*. New York, NY: Holt, Rinehart, and Winston.

Gall, Meredith. 1984. "Synthesis of research on teachers' questioning." *Educational Leadership* 42 (3): 40–47. Education Resources Information Center (ERIC) EJ310029.

Ginsburg, David. 2015. "Rapid release of responsibility: You do, we do, I do." *Education Week*. January 31.

Handler, Jack G. 1994. *Ballantine's Law Dictionary*. Albany, NY: Delmar.

Hess, Karin K. 2014. "The Hess Cognitive Rigor Matrix." April 11. Accessed January 28, 2019. https://www.karin-hess.com/single-post/2014/4/11/The-Hess-Cognitive-Rigor-Matrix.

———. 2019. "'Cognitive Rigor and Depth of Knowledge' and assorted CRMs therein." Accessed October 9, 2019. https://www.karin-hess.com/cognitive-rigor-and-dok.

Hess, Karin K., Ben Jones, Dennis Carlock, and John R. Walkup. 2009. "Cognitive rigor: Blending the strengths of Bloom's taxonomy and Webb's Depth of Knowledge to enhance classroom-level processes." Education Resources Information Center (ERIC) ED517804, 1–8. http://standardsco.com/PDF/Cognitive_Rigor_Paper.pdf.

Himmel, J. "Language objectives." https://www.colorincolorado.org/article/language-objectives-key-effective-content-area-instruction-english-learners.

Hollingsworth, John, and Silvia Ybarra. 2009. *Explicit Direct Instruction*. 1st Ed. Thousand Oaks, CA: Corwin Press.

Hunter, Madeline. 1994. *Enhancing Teaching*. 1st Ed. London: Macmillan.

Karuguti, Wallace Mugambi. 2017. "Analysing the cognitive rigor of interprofessional curriculum using the Depth of Knowledge framework." *Journal of Interprofessional Care* 31 (4): 529–532. https://doi.org/10.1080/13561820.2017.1310718.

Kaufer, Daniela. 2011. "What can neuroscience research teach us about teaching?" UC Berkeley Graduate Student Instructor Teaching & Resource Center. Accessed May 3, 2017. https://gsi.berkeley.edu/programs-services/hsl-project/hsl-speakers/kaufer/.

References

Keen, C. 2006. "University study finds random student selection keep students engaged." *Kagan Online Magazine*. https://www.kaganonline.com/free_articles/research_and_rationale/331/University-Study-Finds-Random-Student-Selection-Keeps-Students-Engaged.

Krathwohl, D. 2002. "A revision of Bloom's Taxonomy: An overview." *Theory into Practice* 41: 212–218. https://doi.org/10.1207/s15430421tip4104_2.

Lafreniere, S. 2013. "Revised Bloom's taxonomy action verbs." August 13. Accessed October 15, 2019. https://www.apu.edu/live_data/files/333/blooms_taxonomy_action_verbs.pdf.

Lee, Albert, Lin Ding, Neville W. Reay, and Lei Bao. 2011. "Single-concept Clicker question sequences." *The Physics Teacher* 49 (6): 385–389. https://aapt.scitation.org/doi/10.1119/1.3628273.

Levy, Ellen. 2008. "Gradual release of responsibility: I do, we do, you do." January 15. Accessed April 12, 2019. Washoe County School District. https://www.washoeschools.net/cms/lib/NV01912265/Centricity/Domain/257/Certified%20Hiring/GradualReleaseResponsibilityJan08.pdf.

Lynda.com. 2019. "Understanding the principles of design." Accessed October 1, 2019. https://www.lynda.com/Design-Techniques-tutorials/Understanding-principles-design/506078/539550-4.html.

McGaan, Lee. 2015. "Questions to stimulate metacognitive reflection and learning." Adapted from K.D. Tanner. 2012. "Promoting student metacognition." *CBE Life Sciences Education* 11 (2): 113–120.

Melder, Logan. 2011. "Wait time in the classroom." Master of Science Thesis, Rowan University. https://rdw.rowan.edu/cgi/viewcontent.cgi?article=1071&context=etd.

Michaelsen, Larry K., Arletta Bauman Knight, and L. Dee Fink. 2001. *Team-Based Learning: A Transformative Use of Small Groups*. Westport, CT: Praeger.

Morisey, Drew. 2014. "How to rap: Introduction to metaphors." Video file. Accessed June 14, 2019. https://www.youtube.com/watch?v=gC9nTZ3uVNY.

NGSS Lead States. 2013. "MS-PS1 matter and its interactions." Accessed December 7, 2018. https://www.nextgenscience.org/dci-arrangement/ms-ps1-matter-and-its-interactions.

Office of Career Readiness. 2014. "Criminal justice standards." Nevada Department of Education. Accessed February 4, 2019. http://www.doe.nv.gov/uploadedFiles/ndedoenvgov/content/CTE/Programs/HealthSci_PublicSafety/Standards/Criminal-Justice-STDS-ADA.pdf.

Oklahoma State Department of Education. 2006. "Priority Academic Student Skills – The arts." Oklahoma State Board of Education. https://sde.ok.gov/sites/ok.gov.sde/files/C3%20PASS%20Intarts.pdf.

Olvera, Gerlinde W., and John R. Walkup. 2010. "Questioning strategies for teaching cognitively rigorous curricula." Education Resources Information Center (ERIC) ED518988. Accessed February 2, 2014. http://files.eric.ed.gov/fulltext/ED518988.pdf.

Pearson, P. David, and Margaret C. Gallagher. 1983. "The instruction of reading comprehension." *Contemporary Educational Psychology* 8: 317–344. https://doi.org/10.1016/0361-476X(83)90019-X.

Petty, Geoff. 2006. *Evidence-based Teaching: A Practical Approach*. Cheltenham, UK: Nelson Thornes Ltd.
Pressley, M., and K. R. Harris. 2017. "Cognitive strategies instruction: From basic research to classroom instruction." *Journal of Education* 189 (1–2): 77–94. Accessed February 12, 2018. https://doi.org/10.1177/0022057409189001-206.
Redfield, Doris L., and Elaine Waldman Rousseau. 1981. "A meta-analysis of experimental research on teacher questioning behavior." *Review of Educational Research* 51: 237–245. https://doi.org/10.3102/00346543051002237.
Riley II, Joseph P. 1986. "The effects of teachers' wait-time and knowledge comprehension questioning on science achievement." *Journal of Research in Science Teaching* 23: 335–342. https://doi.org/10.1002/tea.3660230407.
Rowe, Mary Budd. 1980. "Pausing principles and their effects on reasoning in science." *New Directions for Community Colleges* 8 (3): 27–34. https://doi.org/10.1002/cc.36819803106.
———. 1987. "Wait time: Slowing down may be a way of speeding up!" *Journal of Teacher Education* 37 (1): 4350. https://doi.org/10.1177/002248718603700110.
Sadker, David, and Myra Sadker. 1985. "Is the O.K. classroom O.K.?" *Phi Delta Kappan* 66 (5): 358–361. Education Resources Information Center (ERIC) EJ311711.
Shabatu, Jessica. 2018. "Bloom's taxonomy verb chart." Accessed October 15, 2019. https://tips.uark.edu/blooms-taxonomy-verb-chart/.
Simsek, Ali, and Jale Balaban. 2010. "Learning strategies of successful and unsuccessful university students." *Contemporary Educational Technology* 1 (1): 36–45. Education Resources Information Center (ERIC) ED542214.
South, Justin. 2014. "Figurative language in country songs (and more)." Video file. Accessed June 19, 2019. https://www.youtube.com/watch?v=aVtUbLy-L78.
Southern Cross University. n.d. "Graduate attribute 1: Intellectual rigor." Accessed December 12, 2018. https://www.scu.edu.au/staff/teaching-and-learning/graduate-attributes/ga1-intellectual-rigour/.
Stahl, Robert J. 1994. "Using 'think-time' and 'wait-time' skillfully in the classroom." Education Resources Information Center (ERIC) ED 370885. May.
Strong, Richard W., Harvey F. Silver, and Matthew J. Perini. 2001. *Teaching What Matters Most: Standards and Strategies for Raising Student Achievement*. Alexandria, VA: ASCD.
Teaching Innovation & Technological Support. 2018. "Bloom's Taxonomy verb chart." University of Arkansas. Accessed March 14, 2019. https://tips.uark.edu/blooms-taxonomy-verb-chart/.
TeachThought. 2018. "126 Bloom's Taxonomy verbs for digital learning." Accessed March 7, 2019. https://www.teachthought.com/critical-thinking/126-blooms-taxonomy-verbs-digital-learning/.
The Getty Museum. 2011. "Principles of design." Accessed November 30, 2018. https://www.getty.edu/education/teachers/building_lessons/principles_design.pdf.
The Standards Company LLC. 2008. "Analysis of the enacted curriculum for the Oklahoma State Department of Education for the collection period February–March,

2008." The Standards Company. Accessed February 3, 2019. http://standardsco.com/PDF/OklahomaAlignmentCognitiveRigorStudy_TSC.pdf.

Tobin, Kenneth G. 1987. "The role of wait time in higher cognitive level learning." *Review of Educational Research* 57 (1): 69–95. https://doi.org/10.3102/00346543057001069.

Tobin, Kenneth G., and William Capie. 1980. "The effects of teacher wait-time and questioning quality on middle school science achievement." Paper presented at the Annual Meeting of the American Psychological Association. Montreal: Education Resources Information Center (ERIC) ED196860.

Torbrand, Pepita. 2014. "Action research-questioning techniques in the FE sector: A qualitative study." *Research in Teacher Education* 4 (1): 28–37.

Tourangeau, Roger, and Lance J. Rips. 1991. "Interpreting and evaluating metaphors." *Journal of Memory and Language* 30 (4): 452–472. https://doi.org/10.1016/0749-596X(91)90016-D.

van Someren, M. W., Y. F. Barnard, and J. A.C. Sandberg. 1994. *The Think Aloud Method: A Practical Guide to Modeling Cognitive Processes*. London: Academic Press.

Wagner, Tony. 2008. "Rigor redefined." *Educational Leadership* 66 (2): 20–24.

Walsh, Jackie A. 2015. *Questioning for Classroom Discussion: Purposeful Speaking, Engaged Listening, Deep Thinking*. Alexandria, VA: ASCD.

Walsh, Jackie Acree, and Beth Dankert Sattes. 2005. "How can quality questioning transform classrooms? Questioning to advance thinking, learning, and achievement." Chap. 1 in *Quality Questioning*, 1–21. Thousand Oaks, CA: Corwin Press. https://www.sagepub.com/sites/default/files/upm-binaries/6605_walsh_ch_1.pdf.

Washor, E., and C. Mojkowski. 2006. "What do you mean by rigor?" *Educational Leadership* 64: 84–87.

Wasley, P., R. L. Hampel, and R. W. Clark. 1997. *Kids and School Reform*. San Francisco, CA: Jossey-Bass.

Watercolorpainting.com. 2019. "Design: Principles and elements." Accessed October 1, 2019. https://watercolorpainting.com/design/.

Webb, Norman L. 1999. "Alignment of science and mathematics standards and assessments in four states (Research Monograph No. 18)." Washington, DC: Council of Chief State School Officers and National Institute for Science Education. Accessed January 1, 2018. http://archive.wceruw.org/nise/Publications/Research_Monographs/vol18.pdf.

———. 2002. "Depth-of-Knowledge levels for four content areas." Accessed January 1, 2018. http://facstaff.wcer.wisc.edu/normw/All%20content%20areas%20%20DOK%20levels%2032802.pdf.

———. 2005. "Web Alignment Tool (WAT)." Madison, WI: Council of Chief State School Officers and the Wisconsin Center for Education Research. Accessed January 1, 2018. http://wat.wceruw.org/index.aspx.

Weinstein, C. E., and R. E. Mayer. 1986. "The teaching of learning strategies." In *Handbook of Research on Teaching*, edited by M. C. Wittrock, 315–327. NY: Macmillan.

Wilhelm, Jeffrey. 2001. "Think-alouds boost reading comprehension." *Instructor* 111 (4): 26–28.

Index

Page references for figures are italicized.

action verbs, xii, xxiii–xxvii, 16, 26, 28, 40–41, 96, 99, 108

background barriers, xii, xxxii–xxxiv, 23, 28, 33, 35, 36, 57, 59–76, 99–101
Bloom's digital taxonomy, xxiii
Bloom's revised taxonomy x–xi, xxi. *See also* Cognitive Process Dimension (CDP); Knowledge Dimension (KD)
Bloom's taxonomy (original), x–xi, xxi
Boomer Sooner!, 10n1

Cognitive Process Dimension (CPD), xix, xxi–xxvii, xxix–xxxiii,15, 39–43, 57, 74–77, 79–81, 83, 99 108; analyze category, xxiv, xxvi–xxvii, 9, 40–43, 45, 48, 50, 52, 55–56, 68, 70, 73, 75–76, 80–81, 96, 101, 103, 106, 109–10; apply category, xxiv, xxvi–xxvii, 28, 41, 42–43, 45, 48–49, 52–56, 61, 68, 70, 73, 75–76, 79–81, 101, 106, 110; create category, xxiv, xxvi–xxvii, 8, 41–43, 46–48, 51–52, 55, 57, 68, 70, 73, 75–76, 80–81, 101, 106; evaluate category, xxiv, xxvi–xxviii, 41–43, 45, 48, 50–52, 55, 57, 68, 70, 73, 75–76, 80–81, 101, 106, 109; mapping to instructional methods, 41–43; remember category, xxiv, xxvi–xxviii, 28, 41–44, 47–48, 52, 55, 68, 70, 73, 75–76, 79–80, 99, 101, 103; understand category, xxiv, xxvi–xxviii, 28, 41–44, 48, 52–53, 55–56, 68, 70, 73, 75–76, 79–81, 96, 101, 103, 106, 109–10
Cognitive Rigor, xi–xii, xvii, xxvii, 60–61
Cognitive Rigor Matrix, xi–xii, xvii–xviii, xxvii–*xxviii*, xxx–xxxi
Cognitive Rigor research, xi
cognitive strategies, 57, 99, 105–6; elaboration, 43, 48, 52, 55–57, 63, 68, 70, 73, 75, 82, 99, 101, 103, 105, 106–7; organization, 43–44, 48, 52, 55, 68, 70, 73, 75, 105–6; rehearsal, 41, 43–44, 48, 51–52, 55, 62, 68, 70, 73, 75, 101, 103, 105, 107

Depth of Knowledge (DOK), x–xi, xix, xxi–xxviii, xxx–xxxiii, 1, 11–13, 17–18, 21, 29, 39, 56–57, 77, 82–84, 89, 96; DOK-1 level, xxi–xxii, xxiv, xxvi–xxvii, 61, 83–84, 89, 91, 103; DOK-2 level, xxii, xxvi, 12, 18, 20, 32, 51, 54, 71, 83, 85, 91, 102–3; DOK-3 level, xxii, xxvi, 17–18, 29, 30, 33, 35, 42, 83, 91; DOK-4 level, xxi–xxii, xxiv, xxvi, 11, 13, 17–19, 31, 47, 83–84, 89, 91, 97; impact on homework, 89, 91, 103; impact on student grouping, 82, *83*, 89, 97; impact on wait time, *83–5*

formative assessment, xxx, xxxiv, 77–78, 102; checking for understanding, xxxiii–xxxiv, 46, 51, 63, 76–79, 80, 85–87, 91–93, 102–3, 109; questioning for engagement, xxxiii–xxxiv, 76, 78–80, 85, 87, 91–94, 102–3, 109

Gradual Release of Responsibility (GRR), xiii, 43, 46–48, 55, 68, 70, 75, 106–7
GRAPPLE questioning method, 78, *82*, 83–84, 102
guided inquiry, xiii, 39, 41, 48–49, 55, 70, 75, 82, 110–11

Hess Cognitive Rigor Matrix. *See* Cognitive Rigor Matrix
Hess CRMs. *See* Cognitive Rigor Matrix
Hess Matrix. *See* Cognitive Rigor Matrix
homework, 58n2, 64, 87–91, 103–4

I do, we do, you do, 52–54, 71, 73, 107–8
intellectual rigor. *See* rigor

Knowledge Dimension (KD), xix, xxi, xxvii, *xxix*–xxxiii, 4, 21, 23–24; 28–34, 39, 42, 47, 57, 60–63, 67, 69, 71, 97, 100; communicative knowledge, xvii–xviii, xxix–xxx, xxxiii, 24, 27–36, 61, 98; conceptual knowledge, xxii, xxix, xxxiii, 24–25, 29–36, 56, 61, 66, 98, 111; expansion of, xxix–xxx, 23–28; factual knowledge, xxix, xxxiii, 23–25, 27, 29–32, 34, 36, 79; metacognitive knowledge, xviii–xxx, xxxiii, 6, 23, 26, 29–36, 50–51, 54, 98, 111; procedural knowledge, xxix, xxxiii, 4, 23, 25–26, 29–36, 61, 63, 66; relevance knowledge, xvii–xxx, xxxiii, 12, 19, 24, 26–36, 45, 50, 61, 98

language objectives, xxxii, 17, 19–21, 97–98
learning objectives, xxxii, 16, 18–21, 97
Lesson Content Table. *See* associated sample lesson
Lesson Delivery Table. *See* associated sample lesson
lesson planning flow chart, xxxii–*xxxiii*, 2, *12*, *24*, 39, *40*, *76*, *78*

Metacog Log, 52, 54, 73, 101, *112*
metacognition monitor. *See* Metacog Log
Metacognitive Question Bank, 43, 47–48, 68, 70, 111

pair-share, 33, 52, 72–73, 80, 83, 102–3
proficiency, xii, xvii, xxxii, 4, 17, 29–30, 36, 43, 57, 60–68, 70–72, 74, 79–80, 112

rigor, x–xii, xvii–xxiii, xxx–xxxi, 2, 8, 36, 61, 64–65, 92, 108
Rigor Cube, xvii, xxx, *xxxi*–xxxii, xxxiv, 1, 11, 23, 39, 77

Sample Lesson A (middle school ELA), 6, 7, 17, 29, 42, 66, 91; background barriers, 66–67; culminating activity, 18, 29, 42, 66; formative assessment, 91–92; Instructional Delivery Table, *43*, *68*; lesson content, 29–30; Lesson Content Table, *30*; lesson delivery, 42–47; standard/topic, 7

Sample Lesson B (high school art), 7, 8, 18, 30, 47, 67, 92; background barriers, 67–68; culminating activity, 18, 31, 47, 67; formative assessment, 92; Instructional Delivery Table, *48, 70*; lesson content, 31–32; Lesson Content Table, *32*; lesson delivery, 47–51; standard/topic, 8

Sample Lesson C (high school math), 7, 9, 19, 32, 51, 71, 92, 111; background barriers, 71–2 culminating activity, 20, 32, 51, 71; formative assessment, 92–93 Instructional Delivery Table, *52, 73*; lesson content, 32–33; Lesson Content Table, *34*; lesson delivery, 51–52, 74–75; standard/topic, 9

Sample Lesson D (middle school STEM), 7, 9, 20, 33, 54, 72, 93; background barriers, 72–73; culminating activity, 20, 34, 54, 72; formative assessment, 93–94; Instructional Delivery Table, *55, 75*; lesson content, 34–36; Lesson Content Table, *36*; lesson delivery, 54–55; standard/topic, 9–10

Sample Lesson E (high school CTE), 7, 95; background barriers, 100–101; culminating activity, 96; formative assessment, 102–3; Instructional Delivery Table, *101*; lesson content, 97–98; lesson delivery, 99–101; standard/topic, 95–96

Socratic seminars, xiii, xxxiv, 57, 99–101, 103, 109–10

Specially Designed Academic Instruction in English (SDAIE), 17, 43, 45, 48, 68, 70

state content standards, xi–xiii, xix, xxiii, 1–3, 6, 9, 20, 23; college/career-readiness standards, xxxii; Common Core State Standards, xii–xiii, 2–3, 6–7, 9; Nevada CTE standards, 3, 7, 95; Next Generation Science Standards (NGSS), xi, 2–3, 7, 9, 20, 82; Oklahoma PASS standards, 7–8

subskill scaffolding, xxxiii, 28, 40, 58–67, 69, 71–74

summative assessment, 77

taxonomy table, xxx–xxxi

think-aloud, 43, 45–51, 53–55, 57, 68, 70, 75, 107–9

verbs: action verbs, xii, xxiii–xxv, xxvii, 7–9, 16, 26–43 63, 74–76, 96, 99, 108; alternative Bloom verbs, 40–41; Bloom's verbs. *See* action verbs; question stems, 80–*81*

Writing across the curriculum marking guideline, 67–70